"My Dad Says..."

by John E. Fry

"My Dad Says..."

A Collection of Stories and Experiences of a Time when Simple Joys Filled Each Day as Expressed or Recalled by the Author

Front cover: Plat book drawing of Jacob Fry farm
in Will County, circa 1880
(Jacob Fry was John Fry's great-grandfather.)

Printed and Bound in the United States of America

First Printing: 2000

ISBN
0-9674279-0-8

Acknowledgments

Special thanks to:

Bonnie Klee, who urged my return from a writing hiatus.

Juanita Harr, Dawn Anderson, Marti Palmer, Sharon Michel, Phyllis Wheeler, and Mansie O'Leary for helping this book come into being.

Many friends and acquaintances for their words of encouragement.

My sons:
    Alan and his family, Nancy, Andy, Ember, Erin, Ed, and Adam
    Larry and his family, Mary Lou, Sandra, and Stephen
    Gordon and his family, Debbie, Becky, Brian, Matthew, and Christine
    For their confidence, patience, and support as voiced from time to time.

Finally, I wish to thank my wife, Laurabelle W. Fry (Laura) for her love and countless helps over the span of 56 years.

Table of Contents

About the Author

by J. Alan Fry

J ohn Eugene Fry was born on October 26, 1922, in Chicago, Illinois, to John George and Mabel Rohrbaugh Fry. The young family lived in several homes in Naperville, Illinois, until they moved into a brand-new Queen-Anne-style home at 624 Brainard Street on the east side of Naperville in 1926. He attended kindergarten at the Sergeant Building and spent his elementary years at Ellsworth School. His music teacher, Mr. E. A. Hill, introduced him to the trombone in the sixth grade. His library privileges were revoked in seventh grade because he was such a voracious reader that he would ignore his studies to read.

He attended Naperville High School and attended North Central College from 1941 to 1942. While he attended North Central, he was selected as a member of a male octette that traveled throughout the western United States in the summer of 1941. He was well known for his trombone playing and won many competitions and contests on that instrument. He was the debate champion for all of DuPage County in 1940. During the summers, he pitched bundles, caddied, and weeded in a local nursery. He often painted homes with his father and recalled that many of his teenage jobs involved terribly hard work. He also worked as a service station attendant from the time he was a senior high school student until he entered the service in 1943.

In 1942, he tried to enlist in the Air Corps, but his visual perception was just not quite good enough. He was drafted into the Army in February of 1943 and was transferred to the medical corps and assigned to the 37th Field Hospital. He was introduced to Laurabelle Wileden of Plymouth, Michigan, by his friend Kyle Brand. They were married on May 15, 1943, in Indianapolis, Indiana. He was sent to the Pacific theater in February of 1944 and spent the next 22 months in New Guinea and in the Philippines. He returned home on December 20, 1945. It was his good fortune to have never been seriously wounded or ill while in the service.

Upon returning from the service, he graduated from Cleary Business College in Ypsilanti, Michigan. In 1947, their first son John Alan was born, and the family returned to Naperville. He worked for Dun and Bradstreet for two and one-half years and sold life insurance for a similar length of time. In 1953, he joined his brothers, Jim and Mark, and formed Fry Brothers Realty. In 1958, John began his long career as a land developer when he and his friend, Glenn Vermaat, developed Hobson Homelands. Since that time, John and sons Alan, Larry, and Gordon, have continued to develop many properties including Tamarack Fairways which is a golf course community. At this time, over 2,000 families live in their many subdivisions.

John has served his community and his church in many ways. He served as the president of the Naperville Council of Churches and served on the Northern Illinois/Wisconsin District Board of the Church of the Brethren. He led the building campaign for the construction of the new Church of the Brethren in Naperville. He is a member of the Lions Club and was a founding member of the DuPage Multiple Listing Service. He is a charter member of the Naperville Men's Glee Club as well as the Naperville Chorus. He and his wife now have nine grandchildren and live on four acres in the home they built in 1972.   ✿

Foreword

by Gordon Fry

What a privilege it is to be able to share with you some of the wit and wisdom that has been passed down to me over the past 43 years by my father. Through this collection of stories that he has written, I hope you can get a sense of why my father has been so respected by so many people whom he has helped and touched throughout the years.

Throughout my entire life, I have heard kind words about my father very often. I can best illustrate this with a true story. Last winter, we had a really nasty snowstorm here in Naperville. I was called out to plow snow for the township and had put in 14 hours of work with only a very short break. As I was plowing snow on a street near my dad's house at about 10:00 P.M., a lady came out and asked me if I would plow out her driveway. I said that I was really tired and did not have time. She then told me that she lived alone and had heart trouble. Of course, I was ridden with guilt and agreed to plow out her driveway.

When I had finished, she wanted to give me a check for my efforts so she asked my name. When I told her my name was Gordon Fry, she said, "Oh, you're one of the Fry boys!" Even in my exhausted state, I had to find some humor in the fact that she thought of me as a boy even though I was 43 years old. She then made some very nice comments about my father and our entire family, gave me a check for more than I had asked, and sent me on my way. Later, as I reflected on the incident, I realized that my father's way of treating people with honesty and compassion, even as they did something as simple as buying a home site from him, had stuck with this lady for almost 30 years!

My father has always had a very practical attitude in using a combination of his strong moral values and the influence of his religious beliefs in helping others. He used these same wonderful attributes in rearing his children; and along the way, he imbued in them the knowledge that he loves them. This is reflected in the fact that all three of his sons and their families are highly involved in their churches as well as in the community. If I attempted to list all of the worthy causes in which his family is involved, I would need my own chapter in this book, and you did not buy it to read my writing. You bought it to read my dad's writing. I hope you enjoy *My Dad Says....*   ✤

Introduction
by Larry Fry

To paraphrase Mark Twain, a son's greatest hero is his father. However, when that boy reaches his teenage years, his hero falls off his throne, becomes the town simpleton, and can do nothing right. When that same boy reaches his early 20's, he is amazed at how much his father has learned in just a few short years.

I, too, shared this experience with one major exception. I always knew my father was different from other dads. I knew he could figure out how to fix just about anything or design whatever he needed. He could speed read and seemed to have 99 percent comprehension. He loved to sing in the choir and was very active in the church. He enjoyed hunting pheasants and could aim and fire his shotgun with extreme speed and accuracy. In many ways, he did what other people said could not be done.

My two brothers and I have worked with my father in the family business all of our lives. None of us planned on staying with Dad, and we prepared to enter fields as diverse as our personalities in aeronautics, food science, and accounting. I cannot remember Dad offering salaries, making any promises about our futures, or giving any definitive reasons for us to stay and work with him. He paid for our college educations, cars, and other expenses. We worked hard—after school and on Saturday, all summer, and during school vacations. He was a hard taskmaster but always fair and honest.

As I reflect on our reasons for staying in the family business, I believe it is because each of us realized that he was offering us more than just a job. We were part of a team. Dad always said that he couldn't have been as successful without the hard work of his sons. He gave us an equal voice in the direction of the company and prepared us for the day when the three sons began to run the family business.

Now almost 30 years later, I know I made the right choice in staying with my dad. But only recently, as I read his stories, I discovered a part of his life which was unknown to me. As is typical of my father, it didn't take much work to convince him to share with others the stories he had written for only his immediate family.

I have several selections which are my favorites. Everyone seems to find a story which may not be exactly like his own, but it contains the same theme. I hope you find that special story within these pages which speaks to your heart.   ❀

I, John Fry, First of...

I, John Fry, first of five sons born to George Frederick Fry and Mabel Rohrbaugh Fry, was born on October 26, 1922, at Bethany Hospital in the Garfield Park area of Chicago. My brothers were Robert Paul, Mark Henry, James Arthur, and William Andrew. Basically there are two years between Bob and me. Mark, Jim, and Bill arrived 18 months apart. While I was born in Chicago, our home was in Naperville, Illinois.

In 1922, Naperville was a town of 4,500 people in central DuPage County. Naperville was a better-than-average town located on the CB&Q Railroad about 30 miles southwest of downtown Chicago. Thus the town was blessed with Railway Express service, freight service, and a marvelous commuter rail service. The time to downtown Chicago's Loop ranged from 33 to 90 minutes. The railway coaches were clean (except for soot), well-heated, and ventilated.

Naperville boasted much park land, North Central College, Evangelical Theological Seminary, Nichols Library, a YMCA, a theater as of 1931, and "The World's Largest Manufacturer of Upholstered Furniture"—the Kroehler Manufacturing Company.

The American Legion Post #43 was active. The Masonic Lodge was strong. There were many churches. The high school enrollment for many years was about 400 students.

There also were Centennial Beach, Sportsman's Club, St. Joseph's Orphanage at nearby Lisle, a municipal band and, of course, the usual galaxy of clubs and organizations.

In 1922, my folks rented an upstairs flat on West Jefferson Avenue from Minnie Staffeldt. Of course, I remember nothing of that time.

The years 1923 and 1924—I remember sometime in those two years Bill Boecker and a friend riding past on their horses. I also recall that the Springborn family next door got a new car. It was medium blue with black-painted fenders. They sprinkled it with the garden hose on a bright sunny day, and it left watermarks. They washed the car again and wiped it dry, but it still had water specks.

Another boy and I poured some of my dad's oil and thinner into our sandbox. What followed was my first lesson in cursing and swearing. (My dad had punched cows for several years and spent a year and a half in the United States Cavalry.)

1925—We lived in a two-flat on Center Street. I remember the stairs and the driveway. That's all.

1926 and on—We moved to the new house at 624 North Brainard Street. Now the memories begin to crowd each other in my mind. I remember the coo of the doves on the rooftop; the call of the blackbirds in the big, old pine tree; the baaaaing of Gietzke, the neighbor's goat; the violet bed along the north side of the house; the trains and their whistles; the thunder that reverberated through the big, unfinished upstairs where we boys slept; my dad singing in the kitchen early in the morning; the hard-tired Autocar dump trucks which rumbled up Brainard Street that summer as they fed the huge Rex pavers laying concrete on Ogden Avenue; and listening to the Hankes and Baumgartner boys standing under the street light at Seventh and Brainard singing, "Home on the Range" to the lead of a wailing mouth organ. I didn't realize then how incredibly talented those boys were. We just took them for granted.

No point in trying to talk about everything in the eight years from 1927 on. I was five years old, and I can really remember!

We lived at 624 North Brainard Street until the fall of 1938 except for a year in 1933 and 1934. For a time in those years, we rented out the house and lived in a little cottage on Center Street. Later we lived in a four-room apartment at Center and Sixth Avenue—all in a vain effort to make the mortgage payments.

One evening when my father was not at home, two bankers came and talked at length to my mother. When they left, they had obtained some kind of note and/or mortgage signed by my mother. We were evicted in the summer of 1938 after a terrible time of anxiety and worry. The story of that summer is written elsewhere—it all turned out all right.   ✽

Irrepressible Youth

Youth comes but once in a lifetime.
–Henry Wadsworth Longfellow

Indian Hill

Throughout the 1930's, any good snowfall turned Huffman Street in Naperville into "Indian Hill." It was the best sledding hill ever!

The City Street Department workers closed off Huffman Street and the easternmost blocks of School Street and Benton Avenue. The streets were barricaded from automobile traffic. No sand was spread. Back in those days, cinders and salt were not used. A city dump truck crept along, and two men stood on the load of coarse torpedo sand. The men used scoop shovels to spread the sand with a flinging motion at intersections and known trouble spots throughout the city. However, Indian Hill was never sanded!

> Few, if any, memories are as crystal clear as those spent on Indian Hill.

Following a high-speed belly flop at North Avenue, School Street flashed by. Then, if the frozen, snow-covered street was just right, you could coast across Benton Avenue; and if conditions were absolutely perfect, an occasional sledder ended up at Chicago Avenue. That was a total ride of two and one-half blocks! Of course, you couldn't steer past spots of bare pavement and choose the best path unless you had a Flexible Flyer sled! Any other sled, polished and waxed runner and all, just could not compare with a Flexible Flyer.

The incredible exhilaration of the ride with the wind and frost stinging one's face and the hiss of the runners on the packed snow was all too brief. Then came the long trudge back up the hill, pulling the sled with an old piece of clothes rope. About halfway down the hill, there was an old gravel pit face where the lots were not suitable for home sites. This bank and drop-off was called the "side hill." Really original!

Sometimes, when the snow was really deep, a few *brave* (That's spelled, "C-R-A-Z-Y.") guys would go down the side hill. It usually meant a buckled runner or some type of injury.

Bob Steininger tried it on a Saturday morning. After various shouts of "Okay, Steiner," "Don't hit the rocks," "Drag your feet," and so on, over he went. He didn't get far; he hit the rock! The sled stopped, but he didn't. He did hit the next rock—with his head.

Now we heard a different kind of shout!

"He's dead!"

"He hit his head!"

"Is he breathing?"

No paramedics or 911 in those days. A couple of guys tied him on his sled and dragged him the ten blocks to his home and to the ministrations of his screaming mother.

———————

Dozens, even hundreds, of Naperville residents spent many hours sledding on that hill. There are few, if any memories, as crystal clear as those of the hours spent on Indian Hill.

I never did have a Flexible Flyer.   ✱

Thirty-Five Cent Cap

W hen I was a kid in Naperville, Illinois, back in the days of the Great Depression, virtually everyone—man or boy—owned a hunting cap. Whether or not you went hunting had little to do with the name of the cap.

Most hunting caps were corduroy. They had visors. A cloth-covered button was sewn on the top where the segments of the cap met at the crown. The caps were usually lined with cotton flannel cloth.

Caps may come, and caps may go. I have never forgotten Sam Rubin and my cap!

Ear muffs folded up inside the cap from the band of the cap. Also, ear flaps that folded up on the outside of the cap were tied with a cloth tape which served to tie the cap under the wearer's chin when the flaps were turned down for warmth or protection. The cap covered most of the wearer's forehead as well as the cheeks and the neck.

In really severe conditions, you wrapped a scarf around your neck and tied or draped it across your chest, covering your chin or neck.

Hunting caps of this description are still sold today, of course. I believe they have been popular for many generations.

Along about school time in the fall of the 1938, I decided to buy a cap. I got on my bike and rode downtown to Sam Rubin's Home Department Store on South Main Street. The Home Department Store had a rather typical dry goods inventory as well as a grocery department. I believe Sam and his family lived in a large apartment above the store.

Sam Rubin was a man of unerring judgment in most things. He owned several business buildings in the old central downtown area of Naperville. He understood what it takes to maintain a viable central business district. For example, when asked why he encouraged a Chinese laundryman and his wife to operate a hand laundry in one of his properties, he said, "Every downtown needs a laundry." In the days of starched shirts and detachable collars, how right he was!

I remember when a group of teenage boys went on a YMCA-sponsored camping trip to Colorado in 1936 or 1937, Sam provided much food and supplies at a very favorable cost. At the last minute, he added several #10 cans of plums! The guys did not like them much, but I guess they finally finished them!

Well…back to my cap.

A common method of displaying merchandise was to stack items on large tables with a six-inch board all around. One could rummage through the pile to one's heart's content. I rummaged.

All of the hunting caps were $1.00 each. There were red corduroy, brown corduroy, canvas, duck, and bright red of all kinds. Down in the pile was a rather bulky cap of heavy wool, variegated colors, dull plaid. It was not a common cap. It was my size—7¾. I tried it on. It was warm.

Since it lacked a price tag, I asked Mr. Rubin, "How much?"

"Thirty-five cents," he replied.

A wonderful day! I don't know what kind of wool it was. I do not know who dreamed up the colors. I do know that in the winter's snow and howling winds, I was warm! I wore it for several winters.

———————

Laura and I returned to Naperville in December of 1945. I looked for the cap. She could not understand how anxious I was to find that cap. But we could not find it.

Caps may come and caps may go. All that was more than 50 years ago. All I know is that I never forgotten Sam Rubin and my 35-cent cap!

❉

Buffalo Robe

One winter, for whatever reason, we were without a car.

My Uncle Henry had a Model T Ford pickup truck with an oilcloth top and isinglass side curtains. It ran okay and was thoroughly air-conditioned—naturally.

Our family numbered seven—Dad, Mom, and five sons. The cab of the truck held the parents and two small "Frys." We, the older three, rode back in the truck bed.

I recall one night in particular. We had spent the evening at Grandpa and Celia Rohrbaugh's home at the telephone camp in Warrenville. It was bitterly cold and snowing, and we were five miles from home.

Snuggled down under that robe, we were warm and safe.

So how does one keep from freezing? A buffalo robe! Yes, a buffalo robe! We had a ragged, old, felt-lined, 50-pound buffalo robe. Snuggled down under that robe, we were warm and safe.

I have no idea what became of that robe, but I will never forget how warm we were under that buffalo robe.

Close Call or What?

Summer 1939. A church youth group hay-ride party was held at a farm north of town. Had the usual church "games." Ate something. Then a couple of us went to the barn, harnessed a team of draft horses and hitched up to a hay rack—sometimes called a "bundle wagon" because they were used for carrying loose hay or to take grain bundles to the separator (threshing machine).

And away we went! Singing. Laughing. Throwing hay around. Grabbing girls. In the vernacular of the era—horsing around.

The boy driving the team called out, "Johnny Fry, come up here a minute!" I swayed and slid to the front ladder rack from which a kerosene lantern hung. I could see why he had called out. The left outside tug was unhooked, and the left horse was excited, snorting, and kicking.

I had had a couple of summers of experience with teams and horses, so I knew what to do. I stepped down onto the doubletree as the driver tried to stop the team, grabbed the tug chain, reached back, and hitched onto the doubletree just as someone on the rack yelled. That mare lunged forward in alarm and dumped me under the wagon.

> **The mare lunged forward in alarm; I lost my balance and fell under the wagon.**

The front wheel of the old steel-rimmed wagon rack was right in my face as I frantically rolled away. It caught me, ran over my left thigh and right calf with both the front and rear wheels. It hurt; oh, how it hurt. Guess what saved me? We were driving through an area of soft, black loam soil. Those big wheels just pressed me into the soft dirt.

I had some fancy-looking bruises for several days. To this day, I get cramps from a "leaky" vein in my right calf. Sort of a reminder of a "close call."

❋

YMCA Camping Trip

One summer morning in 1936 or 1937, a three-car caravan headed west out of Naperville for the Rocky Mountain National Park in Colorado.

The Naperville YMCA sponsored an annual camping trip in mid-summer. The tuition was $25; my Grandfather Rohrbaugh paid it for me.

The first car in the caravan was a 1935 Dodge sedan driven by Elmer Koerner, Naperville's bandmaster of fame yet to come. The second car was a 1934 Chevrolet four-door sedan driven by Champ Stokes, Executive Secretary of the YMCA. The third car was driven by Norm Flanders in his 1933 Chevrolet Cabriolet.

In hot midsummer, these three men and their wives were guiding and chaperoning 12 teenage boys on a 15-day trip "out west."

I am still puzzled as to why I remember so little about that YMCA camping trip!

I cannot remember the sequence, nor can I recall the route. I do remember the mohair seats, the wind through the open windows bringing in bugs and dust, and how hot it became with six people per car.

In the 1930's, few western highways were paved. The gravel roads were in good condition. As we drove those hundreds of miles, we encountered on most days large road graders maintaining the roads. Little did I think that in later years we would own several big graders, and that I would become an expert operator!

We slept in pup tents. The ladies did the cooking on Coleman gas stoves and wood fires. The combination luggage and camp kitchen trailer was pulled by Mr. Koerner behind his 1935 Dodge.

I do not remember anything about the food, so it must have been okay. I do remember that we had canned plums, and we didn't like them.

We camped in open fields along the highway. Our favorite campsites were country church yards, county schools, and country cemeteries. There usually was water and at least one privy.

I know we stopped and swam a few times, but mostly I think we just stayed dirty. One thing for sure—I know we all had chiggers.

In the Black Hills of South Dakota, we visited Mt. Rushmore, the presidential monument still being carved in the cliffs. Gutzon Borglum's stone carvers were still working on it.

At Rocky Mountain National Park, we camped in Estes Park. One of the men cut some small pine trees for cook tent poles. Pretty soon a ranger appeared and fined us $35. No more tent poles. We left soon after.

We took a trip on horseback, and then we could not sit or walk comfortably for days. I still do not care much for horses.

At Cheyenne, Wyoming, we enjoyed a big rodeo with dust, crowds screaming, excitement, and a mock Indian fight.

Mostly we rode and rode and rode by car—hot and dirty. But we did a lot of hiking, too. I could outwalk anyone in those days. Years later in the Army, I always walked point. When you walk the point, you can pretty much decide where you walk and set the pace for the whole marching unit.

I think perhaps we mostly rode, slept, ate, pitched tents, sweated, sunburned, and then slept some more. As I recall, we covered more than 3,000 miles on that trip.

I can remember only a few of the campers beside myself: Roy and Bob Steininger, cousins; Sam Rubin's son Al; that's only four of the twelve boys. One of the campers on that trip was Roy Steininger. Seems that no one liked him. He was little, he wanted desperately to belong, and I can still hear him calling as the guys ignored him and did not encourage his company. Poor Roy—he died young. I never had a chance to help Roy—our paths seldom crossed.

I can remember many incidents for most of the 74 years of my life. I am still puzzled as to why I remember so little about that YMCA camping trip!

Steinie's Last Charge

My very close friend, Bob "Steinie" Steininger was my constant hunting pal in the winters of 1933 through 1940. We shot a lot of rabbits, quite a number of pheasants, many squirrels, and pigeons. There were a few ducks on the DuPage River. We let my brother Jim and his friends take care of them!

Steinie and I graduated from Naperville High School in June 1940. I entered the United States Army on February 3, 1943. I attended North Central College and worked first at Hayer & Springborn gas station and later for Lee Nelson at the Pure Oil station. Steinie worked for the CB&Q from 1941 until he was drafted at age 19 in October 1942. He served in the 29th Division in Europe, including D-Day and six months in front-line combat. After he was discharged in October 1945, he worked for Western Electric in Cicero, Illinois, and then for many years for Moore Lumber Company.

After I graduated from college in 1948, Laurabelle and I, along with our infant son Alan, returned to Naperville and soon began building a house. Steinie's dad worked as a carpenter

Hunting with "Steinie"

before the Depression, and I followed in his footsteps. I got advice from Steinie and his dad, John Steininger.

Sometime along in the fall of 1948, Steinie called and said, "Let's go hunting. There's a good tracking snow tonight."

"Okay," I said.

I picked him up at his home early the next morning, and we drove out to the McDowell Farm on River Road. A time later when the sun was about ten o'clock high, we entered the lower end of the old orchard and headed for the big hedgerow behind the farmhouse. Steinie drifted to the north of the fence row, and I held back out of his field of fire, which was toward some brush piles. Years before we had hunted together so many days that we did not need to speak.

Quiet, still, bright—almost serene. Not a cloud in the sky. Suddenly the scene is torn apart by the wildest, tearing shriek I can ever remember hearing.

Steinie charged, gun at port, as he ducked, bobbed, and wove his way into the thin brush and plopped on his belly in a prone position, elbows extended, and gun at his shoulder, ready to fire.

Laughingly, I mimicked and followed, got up, and walked toward Steinie. He didn't get up. He just lay there, cheek on his gun, with shoulders shaking. Steinie was not laughing! He was back in the war! ✽

Sweater of Many Colors

In the fifth grade, I had a sweater. Some sweater! The colors were so loud and the pattern so bold that to look at it casually made one's eyes water. It was so garish that the girls giggled, and the boys suffered from paroxysms of laughter. I just suffered. My mother forced me to wear it to school. One was entitled to ask, "Where did you get that sweater?"

My Uncle George and Aunt Hattie lived in Chicago. Uncle George had a good steady job throughout the Depression years. They were well off enough to shop at Marshall Fields and the other State Street stores in the Chicago Loop. Every fall, we would receive boxes of my cousin Bob's clothes in perfect repair or condition. Cousins Bob and Margaret obviously had completely new wardrobes every year. We were delighted—until that sweater of many colors showed up. I wore it! I suffered!

> We had no girls in our family of five boys, so I never learned what happened to Margaret's hand-me-downs.

We often played 11-inch softball after school. I wasn't much of a fielder, but I could really hit. I got too warm. I removed the sweater and laid it on the ground next to the telephone pole against which I had leaned my bike. After the game, I got on my bike and rode home. When I discovered I had left the sweater, I turned around and went back to get it. It was gone! Now this was just ridiculous! Nobody would steal that sweater—what would they do with it? They surely wouldn't wear it. If you hung it in a closet, all the moths in that part of town might attack! No dog would lie down and sleep on it—the clash of colors would probably give it distemper." In any event, I lost the sweater. I told my mother.

After announcing, "You could lose your head if it wasn't fastened on" (an old accusation), she said, "You lost it on purpose."

I wished I had thought of that sooner! ✱

Easter Sunrise 1939

I have no idea how I happened to have been elected President of the Naperville Youth Council. I guess it just happened.

We planned a Christmas Vespers for the youth. It went very well. The Easter Sunrise Service was the biggest event of our year. There were several girls and a boy or two on the board. They were very willing workers.

We planned the service with great care. It was held at the Methodist Church, and I believe our speaker was Reverend Wesley Westerberg. I think our quartet sang.

The church was full at 6:00 A.M. It was a glorious sunny morning. Everything went perfectly.

Of course, we took an offering. There were very few adults present. As a result, the plates held $29.00 in silver and $3.00 in currency!

He thought we had stolen the money and ran us right out!

The Naperville Candy Kitchen was the next stop after virtually any event or happening. That day was no exception. When we got there, we tried to get Fred Mistici, the proprietor, to take the change and give us currency. "No dice!" He thought we had stolen the money somewhere and ran us right out!

✽

My '97

Whent anyone says "shotgun," and every time I see "Winchester" in print, to me it means '97. At age 15, I was a sophomore in high school and fancied myself an accomplished squirrel, pheasant, and rabbit hunter.

One evening, my dad brought home a very impressive-looking, very battered pump gun, and with a smile, he leaned it in the corner. This very action in the heart of the Great Depression year of 1937 brought a few unhappy comments from my mother. No doubt, she thought of what the $16 for "another" gun would have bought in food or clothing for five growing boys.

After supper, we learned that our "new" gun was a Winchester Model 1897 with a 28-inch barrel and modified coke. That very evening, we took apart the gun and sawed a piece of broomstick as a plug so the gun would handle only three shells. The next evening, we set out with our, as yet, unnamed gun. Dad, the finest shot-gunner I have ever known, pronounced it a "crowbar," but immediately made a couple of near-impossible shots on two cock pheasants which we kicked out of a fence corner. He had proved once again that he could "hit 'em" with anything! Now he handed the gun to me. From that time on, the pump gun was my '97!

Dad had always been a snap shooter, and, of course, I tried to become one also. While I became faster and faster in getting off that first shot, I rarely killed game with the first shot. Time and again, a rabbit or pheasant was hit lightly or crippled on the first shot, and I had to shoot again to kill. This irritated my dad. Shotgun shells cost eight cents each at that time, and each shell was expected to count in terms of game. We were real "pot" hunters.

I finally reached a point where I was getting off two shots so quickly that the reports almost blended. Of course, the first shot was wasted. At this point, Dad took the '97 and handed me my old single-barreled 12-gauge. He didn't have to say a word. We both knew what he meant. Several weeks and many misses later, I was still snap shooting, but hitting!

Came World War II, and my brother Jim inherited the '97. He never really liked the gun and put it in a corner and left it. There it stood dirty and rusting for four years. In 1950, my good friend, Bob Nuckols, took the gun home and cleaned it. He also honed off the burrs in the action. I bought a used stock to replace the old one which had been taped together for many years. Once again, the '97 was a gun!

Today the action or receiver section of the '97 is silver-white from years of handling. All traces of bluing have been gone for years. In extremely cold weather, the action makes about as much noise as the report of a light-load shell. The lead sight is almost worn off, and the fore-piece of the slide handle is deeply scarred. The serrations on the hammer top are almost worn away.

Why don't I retire the gun? I have—three times. In time, I bought a double-barreled sixteen, a double-barreled twenty, and a Model 12 featherweight. I guess in time the Model 12 will replace the '97 in my affection, but the transition will be prolonged. The doubles are long gone, and when using any gun, I miss the positive safety of the visible hammer.

Better shotguns have been and will be made. Modern advancements in gun smithing have refined many features of the '97. Lighter, easier-to-point guns are made. But "shotgun" to me, means "my '97"!   ✷

Tracking Snow

As a youth, two of the most magical and exciting words in my mind were "tracking snow." When I use the phrase, "tracking snow," I am talking about a snowfall ideally suited for tracking rabbits.

A number of things enter the picture. The snow must fall late in the day so that tracks are not spoiled by cattle, other animals, or sun burn. No wind. Wind drifts the tracks shut. Deep enough to take a clean track. Not too warm, but especially not too cold! Rabbits run in the early evening hours. There are always exceptions, but they are basically nocturnal.

To really understand what I write here, you must be aware that I write as a teenager in the late 1930's and early 1940's—say, age 12 to 20. Yes—the Depression years.

You will never realize how much game you walk right past until you have become a good tracker!

Rabbits were heavily hunted. The daily limit was ten, and the possession limit the same. A rabbit weighing two to five pounds was worth one to two dollars as meat. The daily wage for a man in industry or trades was about $3.50. I was paid 35 cents an hour as a gas station attendant.

We had five guns. A little, single-shot lever action .22 rifle with a worn-out ejector. After you shot it, you pried the shell out with your pocket knife. Also as follows:

- A single barrel, cheaply made 12-gauge with a hammer and 32 full choke bore
- A single barrel 410-gauge with hammer and chambered for 2½ inch shells
- A double-barreled 12-gauge hammer gun with 28-inch Damascus twist steel barrels, full and modified
- A Model '97 Winchester 12-gauge pump gun with a 28-inch modified choke barrel. This particular gun had been carried and handled so much that the breech, receiver, and most of the barrel

> were worn silver; no bluing on the gun, just shiny steel. I suppose I myself carried the gun a couple of hundred days. I still have the '97. It jams because of play in the receiver as the result of just plain wear.

Now, back to tracking! The hunter who finds a single track determines the final direction and does not lose the trail is a real hunter. A good tracker does not tromp around. He drifts along and around the area until he finds a single track leading to a likely meeting spot. It is almost as though the rabbit gets tired of running, finds enough to eat, and then rests for the day near cover or a hole and then, nose into the wind, falls asleep.

Back in the days of my youth, there was plenty of cover. Wide, grassy fence rows. Abandoned woodchuck holes. Brush piles near orchards. Pastures and wooded areas. Osage-orange windbreak hedgerows. Wood lots where farmers cut posts and firewood. Grassy creek banks and little tile outlets for water.

We, my brothers, my father, and I, always tried to bring home game in good shape—not all shot up. Whenever possible, we spotted the rabbit in its nest and "popped" off its nose at ten feet or less. When a rabbit jumped, we would wait to shoot, cover permitting, until it was at least ten feet away. That way, as the shot pattern spread, only a few pellets hit home and very few shot tore flesh or broke and splintered bones. We were called "pot hunters."

Modern farming with no livestock, no closed fences, draining and extensive use of insecticides and herbicides, combined with modern harvesting equipment has pretty well destroyed all small game cover. There is small game in towns and cities because dogs and cats no longer run loose. Rabbits especially are plentiful. In fact, it is likely that most people do not regard small game as such and have probably never eaten squirrel, rabbit, pheasant, wild duck, or geese.

You will never realize how much game you walk right past until you have become a good tracker.

All it takes is a good "tracking snow." ❋

Tree Hut

In the 1920's and 1930's, the Park Addition neighborhood was a happy area of kids. One of the reasons for the happiness was the large number of children. In 1934, the 20-block square boasted 128 children from infancy through high-school age.

They were a sizeable group of basically good children. We did have two of the meanest kids in town as well as some of the best kids in town. As I write here in 1998, I realize that most of the mean guys died at a very young age. There are only two bullies left. The rest are long gone—dead, that is.

Bernie had a good supply of nails—not for long!

All of the kids kept busy, and all went to church. My brother Mark and his friends played baseball almost the year around. Dave Berger, a genius, read books. There were about 46 Catholics and 82 Protestants. The kids had frequent discussions about who were better "cat lickes" or "pot lickes." It always worked out the same. We would finally agree that all churches were okay. Then after a short pause, Wendy Fry would say, "But the Methodists are the best!"

The Rechenmachers had 12 children. Dick was one year behind me in school. He and his brothers and sisters all attended St. Peter and Paul. I could play with Dick, but I could not sit on their big front porch or enter their house. If for some reason a Protestant went into their home, special prayers or something were in order. In spite of their exclusionary rules, Dick and I still spent a lot of time together even though from time to time Dick got orders not to spend too much time with "that Fry boy."

There were exceptions. They never objected to we Protestants playing softball or football with them. Also, they did not bother Dick and me when we built stuff. We built forts in the nearby woods. We rebuilt scooters. We made kites. We repaired hordes of kids' toys.

My most remembered days were the time we spent building a tree fort. A row of silver maple trees lined the north end of the ballpark. One of them "forked" about 20 feet above the ground. Somehow, Dick and I climbed to that fork. We decided it was the ideal place for a tree hut fort. We went through the neighborhood salvaging all the lumber we could find. Then we went to the place where the Kroehler Factory burned their scrap lumber. We also got used tar paper from the factory.

One of Dick's older brothers Bernie had pigeons and also helped his dad with rabbits. So, Bernie had a good supply of nails—not for long! We called them spikes and nails. (Later I came to know the nails as 16d and 8d nails.)

We made a removable ladder so that Joe Rechenmacher, "Pete" Baumgartner, and my brother Bob couldn't climb up and tear our work apart at night. Dick and I built the platform floor so heavy and strong that they could not damage it much. The roof was another story. We finally made it all so strong that they could not tear it apart with the tools available to them. Good thing! Bernie was really ranting and raving about his missing nails. We talked about staying up there some night, but we never did.

About this time, my family moved across town to Spring Avenue. After moving, we never saw much of the Park Addition kids. When I returned from the Army and college, I drove past our tree hut. About three-fourths of it was still intact. I always planned on taking a ladder over and climbing up there, but I never did.

Dick reared a family of 12 children. When we talked, he said he had never returned to the tree. In a collision of a Naperville fire engine and a coal truck, Dick and two other volunteer firemen were tragically killed. Really, that accident moved me to write about the last time Dick and I worked together.

In 1950, a number of men in Naperville had neither the money nor the borrowing power to buy a home in Naperville. Among those who come to mind were Harold Callender, Bob Steininger, Dick Rechenmacher, and myself. None of us had any building experience of which to speak. None of us knew any of the building trade. Best of all, everyone, and I mean everyone, told us we could not build a home without a builder. I had one advantage over the others. I had worked for two weeks in 1946 for a stone and brick mason whose name was Ernest Summerfield. I mixed mud and handled scaffolding and watched him work. When we started out, I knew enough to lay the 12-inch concrete basement blocks.

Dick was our mailman, and he stopped to talk. We soon decided to share some labor. What a crew we had! Clarence Jungels was about to join his dad in the heating business. He had not taken an order in his life, and I was giving orders just like I was back in the Army. Harold Callender, a truck driver who knew nothing about building. Dick's brother Leroy. Ex-professional wrestler, night club barman, rent collector, and in due course, he became an attorney and eventually a Federal District Judge. Leroy showed up with knee braces and soon discovered how out-of-shape he was.

The basement was dug. In one weekend, we formed and poured the footing for it. All of the concrete was mixed by hand or in a small mixer. The next weekend we laid up all of the blocks about four courses high and laid on rows of blocks all around the foundation. One or two of the guys quit! All of the house got built! All of the doom-and-gloom people were 1,000 percent wrong!

Some of the people who knew we could do it, helped us. My brother Jim, now retired in California; Emmet Thorland, dying of Alzheimer's disease; Delmar Hosler, retired in Florida; Bob Chadish, died in Korea; Paul Shiffler, died a few years ago; and Ken Eby. Somehow, it all worked out. By the time we got well settled in our new home...guess what? The tree hut was still there.   ✽

The Kite

Dick Rechenmacher and I were the fixers, tinkerers, and builders of the Kroehler Park Addition neighborhood. We built many kites. Most were three sticks and required a tail.

On a blustery March day when we were about 13 years old, we found two bamboo rug poles about one and one-fourth inches by ten feet. We decided right then and there to build a really big two-stick kite. Design was no problem. We had made so many kites that we could eyeball the dimensions. Of course, angles were all done with string measurements. It did not take us long. For the sake of brevity, let me make a builder's list.

1. Two bamboo rug sticks
2. Coffee can full of flour for paste
3. Black waxed upholstery twine cadged from Kroehler factory workers.
4. Lightweight fiber-impregnated tar paper from Kroehler's lumber yard.
5. Three kite string winders and lots of twine so that we could make a triple bridle and three lines.

It took us only a day to build the kite. It was ten feet tall, a really big kite! We then had to get kite tail and help.

Saturday morning brought a strong north wind. We could fly 500 feet! That's all the twine we had on each winder. The crew consisted of three winders and three kids to hang onto their legs so they couldn't get blown away. Of course, we had kids handling the tail and holding the kite. Dick and I were yelling orders. We had probably ten kids from age eight to thirteen.

Dick yelled, "Unwind 50 turns and tighten the lines."

I yelled, "Don't let the tail get caught. Everybody hold tight."

Dick and his helpers got hold of the kite, and he yelled, "I'm going to hold it up." We surely had plenty of wind! The instant the kite was held upright, it flew! Almost straight up! Everyone was terribly excited as the winders paid out their lines in good order. Dick and I were yelling dumb

Sure enough, the six-kid winder team was being dragged forward.

orders like, "Hang on. Don't get ahead. Keep the lines tight." They *all* knew that.

By now, most of us were concerned about being hauled aloft. The fool kite was 500 feet up and out. The lines were tight as anything. Joe Rechenmacher yelled, "It's pulling me!"

Sure enough, the six-kid winder team was being dragged forward. Well, it didn't last very long. By the time my brother Bob screamed, "My string broke!" the other lines snapped.

The kite landed a block south on top of the five-story Kroehler factory building. Now what?

Dick said, "Let's get Joe and Bob to go up the fire escape and throw it off into the street." No sooner said than done.

But it should have been sooner, for just as the broken kite, tail and all, came skittering down from the building and caught on a wire, Police Chief Eddie Otterpohl drove up in the 1935 Dodge squad car.

Dick asked, "What are we going to do? Everyone has run away, and Bob and Joe are hiding on the roof."

I replied in a voice so trembly that I could not recognize it, "We'll just stand here by the kite."

Boy, were we scared! Eddie Otterpohl, resplendent from crushed officer's cap with gold lace braid to big sunglasses to Sam Browne belt to mutton leg pants to shiny black leather puttees and back to the big 1917 Colt 45 on his hip, got out of the squad car and walked over to the by-now-paralyzed pair of us and said, "Johnny, Johnny..."

Shook his head. Got back in the squad car. Drove away.   ❈

Dry Socks

Deceptively warm and pleasant day in April—sunny, a light breeze. Light-jacket weather—for that Saturday morning.

Alan's scouting troop was going on a half-day hike and tracking outing north of Naperville through farm fields, woodlands, and meadows next to Camp McDowell. Alan was dressed properly and ready to go when I asked, "Do you have your spare socks?"

After 15 minutes of tears and objections, he left with a pair of socks folded and hidden in his pant's pocket. By late afternoon, our number one son returned—tired, but smiling.

His mother asked, "Well, did you have a good time?"

He answered, "Yes, and guess what? There are puddles everywhere in the woods where the ground was muddy. We all got our feet wet and cold."

> "What did you do?" she asked.

"What did you do?" she asked.

"Well, when we got out of the wet woods, I sat down on the ground and started taking off my shoes. As I reached in my pocket, the other kids stopped and asked, 'What is Fry doing?' "

Dry socks?!   ✱

Home and Hearth

Home is where the heart is.
–Pliny the Elder

CCC Camp

As he handed the heavy white oval bowl through the fence, the CCC (Civilian Conservation Corps) camp cook said, "Ham and scalloped potatoes." I could see my four younger brothers watching round-eyed as I had the honor of carrying the bowl down to our campsite.

That's right. Campsite. The bank had foreclosed on our mortgage and evicted us from our home. Their actions were not kind.

> **We boys and my father thought we had gone to Heaven.**

Dad borrowed a tent from the Meisinger family. It was a white wall tent, about 12 x 16 feet. It did not have a floor. We also had a couple of pup tents and a cooking fly.

Actually, except for a lack of plumbing, we were quite comfortable. Our camp was in a beautiful, wooded setting. We had plenty of wood for the cooking fire. We walked or drove our 1936 two-door Plymouth sedan across the river to the McDowell farm where we got jugs of milk and water. My brother Mark caught fish every day.

We boys and my father thought we had gone to Heaven. My mother did not share our enthusiasm for outdoor life and primitive camping. Bob, Mark, and I were taken to Naperville Nurseries each day. We worked at weeding seedling beds. The foreman was loud, bellicose, and mean. We were afraid of him. Though my brother Mark was small and not very strong, he never shirked.

One day, the foreman warned, "Be careful with this bed. These are rare plants and worth hundreds of dollars."

On that same day, it was "reported" that he had kicked Mark in the ribs. Big mistake! Seedlings don't do well with many roots missing!

We were paid ten cents an hour, and we worked ten hours. After a few weeks, we refused to work there any more. My mother was angry. She wanted us to keep our "steady" job. Baloney! She just hadn't realized how we were treated.

We were camped about 50 yards from the fence of the CCC camp where I was handed the ham and scalloped potatoes. When the camp was built about 1933, several hundred young men were housed in typical one-story frame Army-style barracks. Their uniforms and equipment were mostly World War I vintage from the bowels of U.S.A. Quartermaster Corps warehouses. They had a fleet of lightweight Reo Speed Wagon dump trucks of current vintage.

The CCC camp officers were a mixture of active Army members and reservists. They did a lot of real manual labor as well as some paramilitary training and, of course, the ever-important close order drill. The people of Naperville were not thrilled. When the CCC men came to town on pass, there was nothing for them to do. Those who were of age patronized the saloons, and we did have a movie theater.

Of course, there were some troubles which ranged from minor incidents to at least one terribly serious criminal offense. All in all, the CCC fellows were probably neither better nor worse than could be reasonably expected.

The CCC built things. Their work was generally done in various parks and forest preserves at all government levels. At Naperville and vicinity, they built bridges, shelters, dams, roads, and related structures in Pioneer Park, Camp McDowell, and in the various other county preserves. The men cut their own timber and beams, quarried limestone, dug gravel, planted trees and shrubs, and on and on. They did a good job. Most of what they built is in good shape 55 years or so later.

Along about 1937, the camp changed personnel. The young men were shipped out, and an entirely new complement arrived. The new men were veterans of World War I. The resemblance to regular army routines was obvious. Some men appeared to be in poor health. Heavy labor was pretty much discontinued. Maintenance chores and somewhat lighter work seemed to be the principal activity. I assume they were indigent or homeless or perhaps alcoholics. It was this particular group who were at Camp McDowell when my family camped for ten weeks in the woods across the fence from the mess hall.

I am not sure, but I believe we received "leftover" food from them every evening. My father related to the men marvelously well. The commander, a United States Army officer, visited us frequently. He was an older, heavy-set man with an air of absolute authority. I am sure he had some firm orders in place concerning the conduct of his men insofar as our family was concerned.

My father could do almost anything, including smiling and laughing when things went wrong. In that respect, I would like to be like him. After "punching cows" for about eight years and eighteen months in the cavalry, he knew all of the little twists needed to make camp life comfortable and healthy, having lived out of doors a major part of his life.

We rode bikes to town—about three miles on a gravel road. We boys often planned things so we could stop at the beach and shower. Mark and Bob caddied at the Naperville Country Club, and I mowed lawns. Dwayne Fry, probably a distant cousin, went fishing with my brothers every chance he got. We ate everything they caught. One day, they caught a big crappie. We had never before seen one. After that, using a little dime-store spinner, they often caught crappies.

In 1918, my mother, Mabel Rohrbaugh, had bought a 20-year pay endowment policy with a face value of $1,000. Somehow, all through the terrible depression years, she managed to pay the premium. Somehow, New York Life was one of the few insurance companies that did not go broke. The policy matured in 1938 after we lost our home to the bank. Mother went to a local real estate agent, Herb Matter, Sr., and said, "I have a thousand dollars, and I want to buy a home."

"You have $1,000?" Herb said in shocked disbelief. "Nobody has $1,000. But I have the old Dissinger house at 230 W. Spring Avenue. It is $3,000, including the adjoining vacant lot, 66 x 166 plus the alley."

Mother said, "I'll give you $2,000 for the house and lot, but I don't want the vacant." The deal worked. Grandpa Rohrbaugh loaned us $1,000 which Mother repaid at $20 per month. But, the renters in our new house had no place to go. So, we were camping!

Still, it all fell into place. Just before school started, the renter left. The furniture stored at the home of Uncle Henry came home to us on

Frank Keller's truck at a cost of $3.00 per hour. We struck camp, said goodbye to the CCC men, and moved into our "new" house. My father walked around the old frame house that had not been painted in 20 years, scraped here and there with his putty knife, slapped the siding here and there and said, "Well, it will last longer than I will!"

We couldn't sleep. The railroad tracks were only half a block away. That monstrous steam engine blew its long-long-short-long blast from the Loomis Street crossing going east and then from River Road going west—just as they passed our house! Open windows did not help either!

In just a few days, school started. We were finally "settled in" at 230 W. Spring Avenue. It had been an adventurous summer, and I have never forgotten our neighbors from the CCC Camp in McDowell Woods.   ❋

Pen in Hand

Pen in hand, my mind goes back some 50 years to the hunting days of my youth, and I walk today where once I walked.

Come back with me to the John and Mabel Fry home at 230 W. Spring Avenue, Naperville, Illinois. Not much of a house. Built about 1840. Eight rooms. Lovely yard and trees with a small barn on the alley. Cement walk went from the back doors of the kitchen and summer kitchen all the way to the barn where there was space enough for a ton of stove coal and room for the car.

The location was wonderful. Three blocks to Naper Elementary School. Five blocks to downtown Naperville. Two blocks to the high school. Seven blocks to the YMCA. Four blocks to the train station. We could walk or ride our bikes almost anywhere we needed or wanted to go. For me, however, the best part of all was quick access to farmland and hunting!

An apple or some graham crackers for energy.

Those were Depression years. One source of food was hunting and fishing. My dad, my four brothers, and I did a lot of hunting and fishing. Let me walk you through a typical day in the field.

During my hunting years, I learned to dress in layers. Typically, underwear, t-shirt, flannel shirt, sweatshirt, wool scarf, light-weight pants, heavy-weight pants, heavy wool socks, and felt boots or rubber boots— depending on conditions. Now came the big, old canvas hunting coats and ready to go. I have always had warm hands, so light canvas gloves.

An apple and some graham crackers for energy. We drank from springs or sucked on icicles.

I usually carried the old Winchester Model '97, 12-gauge pump shotgun that the family shared. Eight or ten shells in various pockets.

Formerly, there was a cattle crossing tunnel through the railroad embankment at Webster Street just a half block from our house. This led to a basically abandoned subdivision and open farmland beyond that.

When I hunted this area, I had a fairly standard pattern as long as I could face the wind. You found very little game or very nervous game at best if you walked with the wind in your back.

More often than not, I met Bob"Steinie" Steininger at about Eighth and North Eagle Streets at 5:30 or 6:00. No conversation. Just took off north, west of the asparagus field (north of what is now Cress Creek), across the Sigmund farm, west along the south edge of Erbs, and on to the pasture land north of McDowell Forest Preserve. Normally upon reaching that area, we would have a rabbit or two.

At the north end of the pasture along the river, a 12-inch tile discharged and flowed as a little stream to the river. There were a couple of scrubby trees, some brush, and a grassy bank. We often stopped there for a drink and lay down and rested for a little while. We never thought about where that water came from—never got sick.

We walked hedgerows, drifted around, and kicked small cover. We were always within shotgun range of each other. By the way, I can still remember some of the subjects about which Steinie and I talked—things like Coach "Joker" Harshbarger, shotguns, his girlfriend Grace, football, cars, the imminent draft into the Army unless we enlisted in the Navy or the Air Corps, big bands, whether or not he and Gracie should marry before his going into the service, and on and on and on. Funny thing—I tried to talk him out of marrying, and within a year, Laurabelle and I were married! He really was surprised and wrote home to Grace.

The days grow short in northern Illinois wintertime. By the time we covered the barley field and worked our way through the big woods, the shadows were lengthening. Hunting coat was beginning to feel heavy. Wind had come around to the west, and the lights of home were three miles away. The cold began to creep across the land, and now we just wanted to get home. Now, the shotguns were on shoulders, and we moved along at a steady, mile-eating pace back to the town. If there was much snow, we took turns breaking the track without speaking as we chose the cleanest corn or bean rows. Unless it was slippery-muddy or terribly windy, we could cover a mile in about 20 minutes.

The street lights flickered into life. An occasional dog came out to bark his displeasure at our incursion before cowering before the tone of our threats.

At our usual meeting place on Eagle Street, we quietly parted and went our separate ways home.

Tired? Sure! Cold? Yes! Happy? You're so right!   ❀

Our New Home

"We are going to build a house."

"We are what?"

"We are going to build a house ourselves."

"Where?"

"I don't know. We will buy a lot."

"Where did you get this idea?"

"Laurabelle, we cannot find a place to rent. We don't have enough money to buy a house. So we will build one ourselves."

She was not pleased.

We were living with my mother, which was not a good arrangement. I was commuting to Chicago on the train.

It might have been better if my mother had not been a packrat. She saved everything! Years later, after her death, my son Alan and I were sorting her things, and he said, "Dad, look at this." He had in his hand a sizable ball of string. Pinned to the ball of string was a note saying, "Pieces of string too small to be of any use." She saved everything!

The long and short of it was that we were living in dreadfully crowded conditions. Poor Laurabelle!

My old hunting buddy, Bob Steininger, was getting ready to build on Brainard Street. His dad was a carpenter and was available to help. Bob worked at the lumber yard.

My father was not a carpenter, and I did not work at the lumberyard.

Bob had bought his lot through J. N. Lehman, a local realtor. I went to see Mr. Lehman

Mr. Lehman, Joyce, said that a man named McQuillen had several lots for sale in the Pilgrim addition. We chose a lot at 817 N. Eagle Street. It was one block south of Ogden Avenue and three blocks west of North Washington Street.

The lot cost $1,050. We had $700 total capital. By the time my brother Jim and I cleared off 30 large trees and built the block basement, we had

> "Why don't you look for some seconds?"

enough money to buy the basic lumber for the frame.

All along, we had planned to borrow $6,000 from the bank or a savings and loan. Mr. Paul Boecker, cashier at the bank, was polite. What he really said was, "You can't build a house unless you are a carpenter. We can't give you a loan."

At the savings and loan, Mr. Germann, said, "No." He too spoke kindly, but could suggest an alternative. He sent me to see a private lender..

I went, but I don't recall even getting in the house.

The real reasons for receiving no loans finally became apparent. I was from the wrong side of the tracks, and my father was an alcoholic. Alcoholism was not a word in common usage then. In a word, he was a drunk.

What now?

The Shiffler family and the Sanborn family were among the owners of Moore Lumber and Supply Company. Soon I owed the Shiffler Brothers and Moore Lumber rather sizable amounts of money.

Paul Shiffler said, "Go see Augie Germann again at the savings and loan."

I will never know just what arrangements or guarantees were made behind the scenes, but when I went in to see Mr. Germann, he said, "We will lend you $4,000 at five percent interest with payments of $40 per month."

We needed $6,000. The $4,000 gave us little more than enough to pay the current bills.

The house was about 70 percent complete.

We proceeded as though we had the money, but we could not afford to have much help.

Soon, we owed several hundreds of dollars each to Haas and Getz, the plumber; Don Hedblom, the furnace man; and of course, a list of bills including new balances for lumber.

Materials and supplies were almost impossible to find. You could not get nails, modern windows, cement, mortar mix, shingles, or bricks.   Sears catalog by way of their order office was a wonderful help.

One day I was talking to Fred Mihulka, an old classmate who, with his father, owned Home Lumber Company in Warrenville. We needed bricks. They were not available. He said, "Why don't you look for some seconds?"

"What are seconds?" I asked.

"Well, sometimes they are crooked bricks. Other times, the color is odd. Occasionally, they might have some cracks." He told me where the Conkey Brick Company had their offices at LaSalle, Illinois.

Laurabelle, the two boys, Alan and Larry, and I drove to LaSalle to the Conkey Brick Company. It wasn't easy to see anyone, but I made it.

The man who saw me was helpful and a gentleman. He directed us to the brick kiln yard at Olney, a few miles south of LaSalle.

From that moment, it was easy! A man met us at the yard. We told him who had sent us and he said, "You are really lucky. Wait here."

He soon returned with a batch of bricks on a fork lift and said, "Here you are. These Red Lefluer bricks came out with a pink cast instead of a solid red color."

Frankly, they were beautiful. Arrangements were made to ship 8,000 of them to our house, and we were billed through Home Lumber. Not only did we get bricks, but we got $80 per thousand worth of bricks for only $40 per thousand! A few days later, a flat-bed semi-trailer truck pulled along the curb at the house, and a husky fellow unloaded the whole load in the parkway. We had our bricks—8,000 of them…

———

We moved in the late summer, about 14 months after we had started clearing trees. No storm windows. No bricks laid yet. Upstairs unfinished. No carpet.

We did have a Thor wringer washer and an old Harrison electric clothes dryer. These things were hard to get. Our Hotpoint refrigerator and electric range were new. We had a very old galvanized steel freezer. It worked!

Others rarely believe that a person can do things "out of his field."

With the exterior unfinished, our oil-burning furnace really labored. We had some ferocious high heating oil bills!

From time to time, we would order a storm window or two from Sears. They had to be cut, trimmed to fit, and then painted. Tremendous help. But still a cold house!

Once we had moved into the house, the work went a little better and somewhat faster. By the second winter, the bricks were on one side and the rear stoop was built. We built a detached two-car brick garage as time and money permitted. We then enclosed the back porch and poured a concrete driveway and curb.

It was a nice house. To this very day, it looks as good as new.

We learned a number of important things.

Others rarely believe that a person can independently do things "out of his field." I have come to realize that it is only because *he* cannot do so. It just might mean that Laurabelle and I are blessed with more practical intelligence and that we worked harder.

At times, bankers merit the names of "flintheart" or "skinflint." Pragmatically and practically speaking, it is often "whom you know."

For the most part, all professional people are available to implement and to expedite your decisions and plans. They are not to be trusted to tell you whether, when, or where to judge or decide. If a professional person is aware and accepts these basic principles, you will usually find them very helpful and cooperative. If not, go elsewhere.

Soon Laurabelle and I decided to purchase a 50-acre tract of land south of town and began to develop land as a family enterprise. We sold the Eagle Street home. Then we arranged for a mortgage. Just hours before the closing of the loan, the bank cut it $5,000. One more time!

Mr. Hageman, the seller, carried back a note, and we got some money from Laurabelle's folks. We were terribly, terribly short of cash.

Laurabelle's folks, Alfred and Alma Wileden, helped unquestioningly. Their loan to us saved the day. For years thereafter, Laurabelle sent a check to them every time we sold a lot. It just worked out wonderfully.

Back to Eagle Street for just a bit…

We learned every little thing about the skills of all of the building trades by doing and watching. That background of experience has been an absolutely marvelous help over the years.

I am reasonably sure that most general contractors know less than I do about construction practices. Their common answer to a mechanical question about painting is, "John, I am not the painter; ask the painter."

I have always regretted that we do not have a family member doing the actual building of homes. It seemed like forever, but we built our Eagle Street house in a year or less. We saved about 25 percent on the price of materials. Our own labor saved about 25 percent. We started out with less than $4,000.

In 1961, the house ended up with a market value of $20,000, and we had only borrowed about $4,000!

But, one more time! We gained a thorough knowledge of the building trades.

In all of my years as a real estate broker, I knew what I was selling.

Herman Muehlfelt and Sons

In 1951, we bought the 50-acre Hageman farm. It was well-drained. Improvements consisted of a gambrel-roofed barn, a 20' x 40' frame shed, an old shop, a two-car garage, and a very modest two-bedroom frame home, all of which were in very poor condition. We needed a better house in which to live!

> I gave him a handshake and $2,500 payable "when he needed the money."

The shed was in the road right-of-way! So Herman Muehlfelt and Sons, house movers from Wheaton, Illinois, were called to the scene to move the shed.

But wait. Let's talk first about *the* house in town. In 1907, a two-story frame house was built on the southwest corner of Main and West Van Buren Streets in what was to become downtown Naperville, Illinois. Dr. Glenn Wolfe, a local physician and an entrepreneur at heart, bought the property and let it be known that the house was for sale and needed to be moved from the premises. I was excited. Laura, the three sons, and I went to see the house. We liked it!

Of course, it needed remodeling and repair. However, that was not a problem. The house had been treated well and absolutely no remodeling or changes had been made. This meant no surprises! I repeat, nothing had been altered or changed. We could see that it could be a lovely country home.

I met with Dr. Wolfe. He agreed to sell the house for $2,500. I gave him a handshake and a note for the $2,500 payable "when he needed the money."

Now comes on the scene one Herman Muehlfelt. Herman and his three sons were house movers. They just plain knew how to move a house!

Herman and I met at the house. We drove the anticipated route to the farm. We had already determined the "load-out" height by counting the rows of siding on the house, using the siding width of four inches as our factor. Of course, he planned on knocking off the chimney. The house would load out at 36 feet.

Utility lines (drops) are all a minimum of 19 feet above the road or street surface. The truly big obstacle was the main feed lines for all of central Naperville. These lines came up along the river across Main Street at the bridge and thence a half block on to the municipal sub-station. They were only 30 feet in height! Oh, boy!

Herman talked the city into agreeing to raise their lines for $2,500. The phone company was reasonable. No big cables. Tree trimming was tolerable. No valuable trees. I think Muehlfelt's bill was $5,000, but I am not sure.

In short order, the crew broke out sections of the basement wall and pushed the big timber "sticks" in across and under the house, laid up cribbing, jacked up the house, attached wheels to the sticks, and the house was ready to go.

Soon the big day came. A huge army surplus Autocar truck arrived. Her name was "Big Ox." In short order, the loaded house was backed onto Main Street and began moving south—right through the heart of town.

As he walked along beside his rig, big Herman Muehlfelt was in his glory. Straw hat. Big cigar. One shirt pocket stuffed with "seegars."

Big Ox went right down Main street across the bridge and out Aurora Avenue. Now, past the big quarry and the high school and south on Plainfield Road. In a few hours, the house was "over the hole," perched on cribbing.

About four months later on November 1, we moved into our just-like-new beautifully remodeled home. It really wasn't finished, but by Christmas time all was complete. ✱

The 100-Year Flood of October 7, 1954

Laurabelle's parents, Alfred and Alma Wileden, lived in Plymouth, Michigan, most of their adult lives. Alfred was a foreman at the Daisy Manufacturing Company, makers of the Daisy air rifle or BB gun.

Laurabelle and I lived in nearby Ypsilanti until I graduated from college and moved to my hometown of Naperville, Illinois.

> As we crept across, I heard Laurabelle gasp. As she looked back she said, "Some of the planks are floating away."

The long and short of it was that in Naperville, we were 312 miles or eight hours from them. In spite of that, we traveled to Michigan often. Typically, we would leave Naperville on a Friday afternoon and return on a Sunday evening. However, Thursday, October 7, 1954, was a deviation from that schedule.

About 1:00 P.M., the radio in our 1948 Plymouth Club coupe stopped playing. In those days that usually meant that the OZ4 tube had burned out. No big deal. At that time, we were on Route 2 just into Indiana on our way west to Route 6 and thence to Lockport, Illinois, and on home.

Soon, as we traveled west, we encountered heavy rain. The road ditches were carrying considerable water, and the underpasses were partially flooded.

About 2:00, we reached Lockport. It was just now sprinkling. As we came over the hill headed down to the canal and on our way to the bridge over the Illinois Canal, we were met by an incredible sight! Houses and buildings near the canal were flooded or being washed away.

The railroad track ballast had been washed out, and the tracks had been heaved up and bent like giant strands of spaghetti, with a few railroad ties clinging to an occasional rail. The rail leading to the big old bridge was in places washed out and gone. It appeared that there was no hope of anything crossing that old bridge for some time to come.

(At this time in my career, I was employed as a credit reporter by Dun & Bradstreet in Chicago. I worked from my home. It was a good job. The knowledge I gained in the two and one-half years in their employ was the equivalent of more than a doctorate in Business Administration and Economics. In the course of my local travels, I had used from time to time an old, one-lane bridge built on wood pilings, timbers, posts, and decks à la railroad span-type design and construction.)

Within minutes I drove to the street leading to the bridge, traversed (crept) through the partially flooded bridge approach and stopped to look. As far as I could see, the deck planks were still in place on the first span of about 200 feet.

I drove very, very slowly. The second span was not as long as the first and looked better. Got across that one okay. Never thought about what would happen if we could not continue across the third span—no place to turn around.

Well, here was the third and last span. The water was level with the deck plants now. As we crept across, I heard Laurabelle gasp. But we made it! Then as she looked back, she said, "Some of the planks are floating away." My guess is that that bridge was totally impassable within just a few minutes! We had just made it.

Sixteen miles to home! Almost drowned the engine at the east branch of the DuPage River. It was a quarter mile wide instead of its usual 50 feet. The water was 12 inches deep on the concrete bridge deck.

When we got to Naperville, we were met by yet another incredible sight. The flood water was over the Washington Street bridge deck in downtown Naperville also. We got across, although the water was inches deep on the floorboards of the Plymouth. We crossed the railroad tracks on Loomis Street and on over to 817 N. Eagle—home at last!

It was still sprinkling. The clouds were ominous. We had stopped at the cab stand on the way home and purchased milk.

We worked quickly to unload the car and get into the house. All seemed well. We closed the front door—and the sky fell! Rain and more rain! It was reported later that five inches of rain fell in just half an hour, in addition to the earlier fall of five inches.

The only leaks in the house were in the basement and around the bottom of the chimney. My calculations on "setting the grade" of the house when I built it proved correct, and although there was nine feet of water a block away, our floor drain carried away our water.

However, there was pressure from the water in the super-saturated soil around the wall, and water was squirting out of the well and chimney footing. I grabbed a star drill and heavy hammer and enlarged the hole from which the water was squirting. Laurabelle was not happy. She said, "You're going to fill the basement with water." Thankfully, the drain handled the water okay.

Many basements in Naperville collapsed. Hundreds of homes were flooded and damaged.

All of the government flood maps indicate October 7, 1954, as the date of the "100-year flood." As for me, I had only seen one heavier rain. That was on Luzon, Philippine Islands, in 1945. (I have written about that elsewhere.)

Almost all of our friends and neighbors suffered flooding and water damage. Now they knew what I had in mind when I set the foundation two and one-half feet higher than the walk and built the terraces and the stone wall. I had, in my judgment, set the grade high enough to be "out of the water," but to make it all work out required terraces and an additional retaining wall along the driveway.

We did not have the $3.00 needed for stones. Instead, when we went for rides in the country, we picked up stones from fence rows along the road. Just loaded them in the trunk and hauled them home. As the stones accumulated, I laid up the wall—one section at a time. Beautiful wall! No cracks!   ❖

The Animal Kingdom

*Animals are such agreeable friends;
they ask no questions,
pass no criticisms.*
–George Eliot

Blinkie

You haven't lived unless you have heard a real, live English bulldog growl!

Blinkie was an old, beat-up white veteran of many a battle with both dogs and automobiles. His basic snuffling English bull visage was considerably altered by the healed and scarred tears and bites that had left his ear sort of shredded. One eye was almost completely closed. The other eye was sort of red. His right hind leg was crooked and bent. All in all, he had the appearance of an old, old gladiator. His owner, Mr. Bond, was a florist. He grew snapdragons and orchids, and he sold them at wholesale.

The Bond home was a lovely Swiss chalet on a large, double-sized corner lot. Across the street, the twelve greenhouses covered about six lots adjoined by more vacant area for coal, cinders, potting soil, flats, trash, etc.—the myriad stuff needed to run a greenhouse.

The area just described comprised Blinkie's territory or turf, and he vigilantly guarded every inch of it.

I do not know if he loved or hated bicycles; he certainly was attracted to them! When he came out into that street snarling, growling, and barking, it was terrifying.

Fortunately, his sideways, limping gait slowed him down. If he was not out in the street waiting for you, a high-speed entry with feet propped up by the handlebars would get you past him. If Blinkie *was* in the street, you just went around the block!

On hot summer days, he often lay sleeping on the cinder sidewalk along the greenhouse in the shade of an evergreen shrub. My heart always hammered when I sneaked past while he snored. If the snore changed to a snuffling snort—get going!

Really, all of this is by way of a character sketch and background. It

> **A high-speed entry with feet up by the handlebars would get a bicyclist past Blinkie!**

is time to tell you the tale of Blinkie's crowning achievement.

In the front yard of the house just north of the Bond home stood a huge, long-needled, black pine tree. The trunk was probably 16 inches in diameter. The tree itself was taller than any home in the neighborhood.

Blinkie was an individual of very strict habits. Every morning at daylight, he came out of his house, stretched, and left on patrol of the perimeter of his territory. Where was his first stop? You guessed it! The stately pine tree. Circled it. Sniffed it. Made a sideways approach. Lifted his good leg, and left his first offering of the day.

It took Blinkie about 12 years to kill that tree. Can you imagine how he must have growled and snarled when *his* old pine tree was cut down!?

❉

Bobcat

I drove a Ford F250 Super Cab pickup truck most days. A couple of years ago on a hot summer day, I drove into the yard at the Myers farmstead. I was there to see if they had a certain size culvert in stock.

I stopped about 20 feet from the adjoining cornfield and unlatched the door of the truck. Before I could step out, a big cat walked out of the cornfield about 15 or 20 feet from me.

This broad-faced, check-striped, tan-and-brown ragged bob-tailed cat with large, pointed ears just stood and looked at me. I was impressed. The cat was about three feet long. At the shoulder, it stood about two feet tall and at the hip somewhat shorter.

Finally I said, "Hi, how are you?"

With independent disdain and without a single blink, the cat turned and stepped back into the tall corn.

> With disdain and without a single blink, the cat turned and stepped back into the tall corn.

Over the years, I have tracked, observed, hunted, and at times, shot much small game. I have tracked fox, watched beaver, caught muskrat unaware, sighted coon, possum, groundhog, coyote, squirrel, skunk, wolf, deer, antelope, sheep, and on and on.

All wild animals I have mentioned are basically shy, distrustful, and fearful of man. But the big cat with measured diffidence seemed not at all fearful or shy.

I drove straight home. I walked straight to my bookshelves and chose a book. I turned to "bobcat" in the encyclopedia and learned that they are to be found in all of the lower 48 states and Canada. The cats are largely nocturnal and quite fearless.

I have only one problem with "my" bobcat. Most folks can't believe I really saw one right here in northern Illinois. Oh, well! ✽

Bullheads in the Rain

Yes, bullheads in the rain! My mother said, "I like bullheads best of all fish." She would also mention, while on the subject of wild game, that she liked the front legs of roasted rabbit, squab, and pigeon breasts.

Since her husband and five sons were all hunters and fishermen, we ate a lot of wild game. Remember, these were the Depression years.

Back to "bullheads in the rain." Bullheads are gregarious. Not only are they churning at most times, but they are particularly so when it is raining. They gather in a circle or fan-shaped formation like the spokes on a wheel, all facing the hub. The key to catching bullheads is to find where they are. This requires real vigilance in spotting where you pulled out the first fish. If you can dip the worm-baited hook and line in just the right spot, you are "in business."

Another peculiar phenomenon is that bullheads from a given circle run to a same size. We always assumed that catches of the large-sized fish were less numerous, simply because there were fewer of them.

Now, back again to our subject. Bullheads do not like fast-running water. They don't like a wind-riffled surface. When the sun is bright, they will move to an area where the bottom is a little deeper. What they really like is still water and gentle rain. For some reason, they begin feeding heavily—biting—in the quiet minutes just before the fresh wind of approaching rain is upon them. My dad always figured that those few minutes just before it rained too hard were the most productive times.

We surely had fun fishing for bullheads one afternoon as the rain came up the east branch of the DuPage River. We caught 32 ten-inchers! Bonanza! You know, one of the nicest things about fishing with Dad was that he always cleaned the fish.

You don't really know what I mean unless you have skinned a few bullheads. So, let it rain! ✳

The Grey Mare

John Erb was a good friend; I knew him all of my life. Way back before World War II, I pitched bundles into his threshing ring. In later years, he had a real estate license, and we made some good deals together.

Shortly after we bought the Hageman farm, he stored some hay and oats in our barn, ran a water hose from the house to the pasture water tank, and then delivered to our keeping a pony and an old grey Tennessee Walking Horse mare.

I asked, "What's going on?"

He said, "They're free."

I said, "I don't want them."

We just thought the old grey mare had been gaining weight!

But our sons enjoyed having them, as did Laurabelle, so I reluctantly agreed. "Oh, well," I muttered, "I can always get him to take them back."

Erb said, "The mare was bred, but she didn't take—must be too old."

Several months later, Larry went out to the pasture to feed the stock and saw a foal! He ran all the way to the house, burst in, and shouted, "A colt! There's a colt in the pasture!"

Sure enough! That old mare had dropped a big, black male foal. How sneaky! We just thought she had been gaining weight!

The next day, Sunday, we met at church, and I told Erb about the foal. He just kept saying, "Nooo. Noooo—can't be."

His wife Ruth called and said, "Johnny, he didn't have any right to give that mare to you. I own her."

I told her to talk to her husband.

She must have done so, for a few days later, he saddled up the mare and rode off down the road with the pony and colt!

My friend!   ❋

"Kinda' Like a Miracle"

Back in 1959 when our son Gordon was three years of age, we got our first dog. The dog came to us by way of a chance encounter with a friend. Our three sons named the dog "Cappie" after Captain Midnight, the hero of a radio program to which all of our sons listened. Cappie was a black Cocker Spaniel. He was bright, quick, obedient, and great fun.

A good friend, Mrs. Borst, lived a block south of us on Eagle Street. Mrs. Borst was an older lady, our frequent babysitter, and our friend. The three sons never tired of being with her and her dog Freckles. Our son Larry says she was a surrogate grandmother for all of the kids on the block.

On the day we brought Cappie home, Mrs. Borst walked up Eagle Street to our home to eat dinner with us and stay with the boys for the evening. When she stepped into the living room, Gordon burst into the room and exclaimed, "Guess what we have?!"

She replied, "How can I guess? I don't have a clue."

He replied, "It's kinda' like a dog."

"Well," she said, "Is it a dog?"

"Yes!" said Gordon. "Come and see him. He's out back in his new doghouse!"

———

Gordon viewed getting a dog as "kinda' like a miracle," and so it was! Now to our title.

As our director and various of us recall the story of the Naperville Men's Glee Club, it's *kinda' like a miracle*. Isn't it great that we can all believe in miracles? How about:

- the first meeting and rehearsal with 22 men present
- the initial congeniality that became camaraderie and seems to be ever stronger
- the wonderful respect between the Glee Club and the director

- the broad spectrum of experiences in the community
- the hosting of the Naval Academy Glee Club
- the hosting of the Miami of Ohio Glee Club
- the hosting of the University of Illinois Varsity Men's Glee Club
- the Waubonsie Men's Glee Club
- the concerts in the park

We could all, as members, make a list of Naperville Men's Glee Club miracles.

Finally, we all marvel at ten years under the inspirational directorship of Bonnie Klee and say, "It's kinda' like a miracle!"   ❋

The Stallion

My dad punched cows near Broadway, Montana, from about 1908 until enlisting in the United States Army Cavalry. After 18 months of service, he received his discharge in 1918 and returned to Naperville-Plainfield. He and my mother were married in 1920 and proceeded to have five sons in the next ten years. My mother often said that she would have had two or three more if it were not for the Depression.

Many of my most vivid memories go back to those years from age eight through high school. Weather and other involvements permitting, my dad and two, three, or four sons went fishing or hunting. We often stopped at the Meissinger Farm on the DuPage River near what is now the Gartner Road bridge. The farm was graced by many oaks and elms. All along the front circle drive was a partly fenced drive. The open area was about the length of a football field.

Alice and Dan Meissinger lived in the wonderful big farmhouse. Bill was a confirmed bachelor, and I suppose in his fifties. He drank sociably and worked on the farm for Nick Modaff, who later married Alice.

On a typical Sunday afternoon, several of us sons and my father would walk the three miles from our Park Addition home to the river and the Meissinger farm. There, in season, we fished for chubs, shiners, carp, and an occasional crappie or rock bass. We hunted rabbits most of all. In the average winter, we shot over 100 rabbits. Of course, we also got squirrels, pigeons, and pheasant. There were very few ducks and no geese.

Many, many people hunted as we did. Wild game and fish were important sources of food. Often, Old Bill would give us a ride in his Chevrolet. He was too tight to give us a ride all the way home! Sometimes, my mother came, and we would ride home in her Model A Ford.

In all seasons, we often waded the river near the spring. If the water was high, Dad would take off his shoes and socks to carry us one at a time.

One golden afternoon, when there was little to disturb the day, Bill, my dad, Bob, and Mark were standing at the back of the porch gate. Bill and Dad were sober as they had not gone downstairs to taste the new wine in the cellar. As we boys stood and listened to the men talking, the sound of a horse loping could be heard. Moments later, Fred Harter rode into the yard on a magnificent grey or strawberry roan stallion. As Fred reined to a halt and dismounted, the stallion stomped restively and blew and breathed on us in turn. He would not be petted.

It turned out that Fred, the horse trader, had obtained him for a local businessman who loved horses. On this wonderful October day, he had taken a little ride as he made plans for the horse.

Old Bill, knowing that for years Dad had punched cows and broken wild horses as well as his stint as an adjutant in the U.S. Cavalry, turned to us. He said, "Ride him, Johnny."

Dad in his cow-punching days

"Naw," my dad said, "I haven't been on a horse since I left the cavalry in 1919."

"Aw, go ahead, Johnny. Ride him!"

Fred, the horse trader, said, "It's alright with me, if you think you can stay on him."

Now we three boys piped up, "Ride him, Dad!"

Finally Dad said. "All right. Stand away while I check his saddle." (I now know that the saddle to which he made reference was an ornate brown leather western saddle—quite obviously a like-new, very expensive saddle.)

Dad held the bit as he talked softly to the horse and rubbed his neck and forehead. I could not hear what he was saying. Then Bill or Fred held the horse while Dad adjusted the stirrups and loosened the bit a little. All of this took some time; I had worked regular farm horses at harvest time, we had never spent all of this time harnessing up the team. So, once again, why doesn't he just ride him?

Johnny Fry, your dad, Johnny "Happy" Fry is about to show you.

The beautiful stallion now stood quiet, but restless. Suddenly, Dad was in the saddle, leaning far back like a cowboy. With Dad's hat slapping the stallion's neck, the horse gathered himself suddenly, and, at a dead run, cut across the drive, galloped to the far corner of the yard. Dad was yelling a wild yipping yelp.

As they approached the far corners and as the stallion reared straight up, front feet slashing the air and back feet dancing a brief staccato, Dad's yips changed to an even louder yell as the stallion screamed, returned to all four feet and came across the yard whinnying and running so hard that his belly almost touched the ground. I was scared.

I think we were all frozen in tableau as the thundering horse bore down upon us. But all was in control. Dad's feet came up almost to the stallion's neck as the horse sat back with his haunches almost on the ground and front feet planted. The sod was flying.

Faster than it can be told, Dad was out of the saddle and standing by the stallion's head. Now he was talking again, "Easy, boy. Easy, boy. Steady. Steady." Dad rubbed his hat on the stallion's neck. Soon the horse stopped quivering, and, with a low nicker, he turned to the man who had seen what "Ride him, Johnny," really meant!   ✳

Dreaming

I have always dreamed of having a place, where shotgun over arm, I could just walk and look and think. I dream of stepping around the corner of the house, jacking a shell into the chamber of the Winchester '97, and, after letting myself through the pasture gate, just drifting along the open woods.

Then I could stop and look to the alarmed crow or hear the sounds of the chattering red squirrel. Further along the way, I would move slowly along an old fence row and watch the cardinals flit from Osage orange to mulberry tree.

"Does he see me?"

I would silently skirt the hedgewood where, in season, the hedge apples lay in scattered profusion among the fallen leaves and thorny windfall branches.

On an autumn day, the lower pasture pond would seem mirror-like, bordered by the golden willows. Silent as a ghost, I'd drift upwind, as a big cottontail with eyes wide, quivers in alarm as he asks, "Does he *see* me?"

I'd move wraithlike and leave him undisturbed. In another session, I would pop off his nose and enjoy roast rabbit that evening!   ✽

Horse-Pulling Contest

Along about 1937 in the hot part of the summer, Scout Troop 81 was drafted for a day's duty at McCormick's St. James Farms. The assignment was simple. We were to direct and park cars in a large stubble field until about noon. At noontime we would eat hot dogs and beans and be dismissed from further duty. Exciting, huh? Well, just you wait!

Turns out we were to see a horse-pulling contest. A hard, black dirt track had been graded and rolled in the stubble field. A very heavy steel sled, not unlike a toboggan with a heavy yoke chain rigged both front and rear, lay shimmering in the heat. It was called a "stone boat."

I always figured it was called a stone boat because when farmers picked up stones to clear the fields in the spring, it could be loaded with no lifting required. Roll...push...drag... sweat...strain—just to get the stones loaded. The whole affair was, of course, pulled by a team of horses or mules. But, with mules, you couldn't overload the boat. When it got too heavy, they quit pulling, and that was that. Horses can be overworked until they drop. They are usually dumber than mules.

> The team only has ears to hear him as the horses nudge and lean into him.

Now, how did all of this work? Well, just imagine it all as I tell you. Every ten feet along the track, a numbered sign was attached to a stake. A volunteer stood at the stake, ready to step onto the boat as the team pulled past that position. I believe there were 40 numbers on each end of the track. There was already a huge block of concrete in the center of the boat. The idea, of course, is that as the boat is pulled along and the volunteer steps aboard, the load increases quickly.

Now, to explain the planned "pull." A teamster backs his team up to the clevis and pin on the pull chain and drops the doubletree in place. Some teamsters talk softly to their animals as the team leans into their collars. Other teamsters yell like Comanches right off the bat. Many of them whistle. All of them walk right behind the team, on the left side.

Now, they are moving out easily. The horses stand almost full height. Leaning their weight into their collars, they start the load. Now comes the teamwork and the skill of team and teamsters.

The horses are on the verge of lunging. No two horses dig in at the same time. Rather, they pick a steady rhythm of one, two, three, four...one, two, three, four...as the boat moves along, and as the volunteer steps on board and the load increases, every hoof comes down with the force of a mighty sledgehammer! Each head goes down! Neck arches up! Belly goes down until it almost touches the ground. Ears stand up and forward. Tails stand straight out. Eyes bulge. Mighty muscles ripple and bunch, ripple and bunch, ripple and bunch. Chests heave. Breaths whistle. Sweat and lather literally fly.

The teamster talks to his team as he at first holds them back to their best pulling speed. Then literally caught up as one unit of strength and beauty, comes the word, "All right, Bill; all right Tom." The pull on the reins lessens and then makes the smooth change as both horses begin to tremble and almost heave in the traces. As one horse begins to lag, you hear the teamster say, "Bill, Bill, Bill, Bill..." The moment is at hand.

The teamster comes back on the reins just a little and as the boat stops, the team comes to a smooth halt as the teamster praises them for a job well done. They only have eyes to see him, but most of all, they only have ears to hear him as with lather-flecked, flared nostrils they nudge and lean into him. Finally, words fail to convey the connection which they, the team and teamster, so obviously feel.

————————

The pulling teams on that summer day at St. James varied in size and weight. In later years, I learned that the horses weighed from 1,800 to 2,200 pounds. They were Belgians, Percherons, Clydesdales, and various crosses of these breeds. No matter the breed or color, those horses were a thrilling, magnificent group of beautiful, beautiful animals.   ❋

Pal

Pal came to be a part of the Fry's household at 624 N. Brainard Street in about 1934. He was a black-and-tan dog. He had medium-length hair. I suppose he weighed about 35 or 40 pounds. Pal was quick and bright, and he could run like the wind! He, of course, had the run of the house. Hunting rabbits with my dad was probably Pal's happiest times.

At about 5:00 A.M. on any given day, my dad was singing in the kitchen while frying up a big breakfast for himself and Pal. All of that activity did not deter his listening to radio station WLS. Dr. John Holland, Dolph Hewitt, Lula Belle and Scotty, Red Blanchard, and the rest of the barn dance crew were on at that early hour live or by way of transcription or "live" guests. I believe almost everyone listened to WLS.

> "So long, Pal."

Dad and Pal were real "pals." My father worked many long hours. Sometimes, whatever the reason, he got home after supper.

Pal paced the floor from dark on as he obviously worried about Dad's arrival time. Suddenly, he would bark sharply and run to the back door. That meant that Dad was at the corner. Two or three minutes later, the back door would open, and there was so much excitement you would think they had been apart for ages!

If Dad was sleeping off a drunk, Pal would lie down beside him and look terribly sad. He seemed to know something was wrong.

Pal was great hunter in the few years that he lived. One evening Dad came home cold sober and told us Pal was dead. He had jumped over a corn row and into the shot pattern of the 12-gauge shotgun just as Dad shot "over" him. The accident occurred five miles from home.

The weather was severe, I insisted that Dad bring Pal home so that I could bury him. Dad made that long, cold walk yet that night. I buried Pal under the tree in our back yard. "So long, Pal." ❁

Oscar

I do not know how many thousands of years Muskovie ducks have been domesticated. I supposed for at least 5,000 years.

Oscar, a big black-and-white Muskovie, came to us with a slightly stained reputation. His farmer owner gave him to me free of charge. He even stuffed him into a big burlap sack and delivered him to our yard.

"What is so unusual about a duck?" my son Gordon asked. "He's just a big fat old duck. I'm naming him Oscar." As it turned out, he had earned his reputation.

Oscar, it turned out, knew every living thing was a duck. Furthermore, he feared no one or nobody. If men came in to work in the repair shop, he came in with a baleful eye, cocked head, and hissing his right to be one of the men.

You see, Oscar had a secret. He knew that everybody was a duck! As a result, he got into occasional trouble.

For example, he argued with cars, trucks, and tractors. When he came out second best, he would drag himself under the pine tree at the shop door. There whoever noticed him would fill his water dish. Everyone fed him. He would eat almost anything the workmen gave him. In time, he would drag himself out and go lie in the sun.

The old character knew perfectly well that he was far too heavy to fly. But, he flew anyhow. His forays in flight were a real venture to behold. Just finished molting, he would launch out into the pond at a terrible expenditure of energy to get off the water and fly. Now what?

Oscar knew he had to get enough altitude to return for a water landing in the pond. With a huge whooshing of wings, he could gain the altitude for the silo and big barn. Now he was back down to about 30 feet, and, as a pilot would say, "on final."

Wings frantically flapping, he crossed the back yard, as he flared, and with all of his might made one of his now famous controlled crash landings. He, of course, sank clear out of sight. As he emerged and paddled to shore, he was a picture of exhaustion and ready to rest at the water's edge. Soon, when he got his breath, he clambered up the bank and collapsed in the grass where, wings folded and hunched down like a 20-pound ball, he fell asleep.

Oscar lived with us for a couple of seasons. He slept in the barn where he ate, drank, and kept a protective eye on the cattle. Still, Oscar's finest hour was yet to come.

Close to the old homestead was a large granary and corn crib. We tore it down and salvaged most of the lumber. Finally, we were down to the foundation and concrete floor. I got the job of breaking up the foundation and hauling it away. I was using a J. I. Case Co. Model 1150 caterpillar tractor with a loader. I dug into a corner of the old wall and floor, and everything went crazy. Rats, rats, and more rats.

The rats ran up the tractor and right on me. They boiled out of the wall like the rats of the Pied Piper. I yelled for the dogs, but they were goofing off somewhere. They knew they were to help anytime we yelled, "Rats!"

One helper showed up—Oscar! By now, the hundreds of rats had ganged up and headed for an old fence. With beak open, wings spread, and neck stretched forward, Oscar waddled into the fight. He killed at least five of them as he snapped their backs and then tore them apart.

Well, one day Oscar disappeared. He came out of the barn badly frostbitten, and the men in the shop decided he should go.

You know, sometimes, I miss him.

They Called Her "Lady"

When we bought the 50-acre Hageman Farm, we agreed to adopt their old dog. Lady was a liver-and-white colored female. I suppose she weighed about 40 pounds. Her ears were a little tattered, and one eye seemed dim. When we took possession on the agreed date, we didn't see Lady anywhere.

The next day I heard some whining and crying from the garage. I slid back the door, and that old dog charged me like a tough, old alligator. I ran, and as soon as I was far enough away, she returned to her bed and curled herself protectively around and over her six puppies!

Lady walked down the walk, stopped, and playfully flopped down with her head in my lap. She had finally come home.

We could not move her, but we did get close enough in that gloomy back corner to discover that her *puppies* were in fact six smooth stones each about the size of a small grapefruit. Her soft, whining cry was enough to break your heart. The former farm owner had "taken care" of her newborn puppies by drowning them.

I confess to being soft-hearted, but that muted cry and fierce bark when protecting her *puppies* was hard to take. She would not come out and would not eat. She just cried.

I called over the farmer's wife and said, "Feed the dog and come back as often as needed or the dog will have to go." She came over and brought a coffee can half-filled with oatmeal, and Lady ate it!

About the fifth day, Lady came out of the garage in the evening, and I bolted the door shut behind her. After another day or two, she ate whatever my wife Laura brought to her. She began to look better as her milk dried up and after she rolled around in the grass. And so it went.

In her time with us, she had two litters of beautiful pups and reared them. Descendants of Lady's offspring are still in the neighborhood.

Lady was old. I suppose 15 years or more. She was a wonderful watchdog. She could not hurt anyone because she didn't have enough teeth. However, her snarl, growl, and hoarse bark were enough.

In time, as Lady grew older, her teats swung low and a tumor grew in one. It did not seem to bother her. The old girl slept in the barn or under the side porch. When the weather turned bitterly cold, she slept on the basement steps landing. When someone started down the stairs and accidentally stepped on her, you never heard such a fuss in your life!

Well, the days and years flew by. She finally came to know and love us. One day at lunch time, several of our people and myself were sitting on the grass in the shade. Lady walked down the walk, stopped, and playfully flopped down with her head in my lap. She had finally come home.

One afternoon soon after, I watched her limp down the walk and fall. The old girl was almost too weak to climb the stairs, and she did not eat much. I said to Laurabelle, "Honey, I am going to take Lady to the vet. I hope he can patch her up a little." Laurabelle started to cry as I got a lead line to use as a leash.

She told me much later that as the dog and I looked back, she and Lady knew that Lady was never to return. Lady whined and cried softly all of the way.

When I arrived at the Aurora Vet Clinic, I led Lady down the hall. The crusty old vet looked grim as he felt the tumor, looked at her teeth, discovered she could no longer hear much, and then said, "She is in pain all of the time. Do you want to take her home or do you want us to take care of her?"

After all these years, I still miss Lady.   ✸

Men and Machines

One machine can do the work of 50 ordinary men.
No machine can do the work
of one extraordinary man.
–Elbert Hubbard

First Earthmover

When Laurabelle and I decided to start subdividing land into country lots, we knew a lot about selling lots but very little about building them.

We had 50 acres of land. In May of 1961, we completed the remodeling and restoration of the little farmhouse on the property and rented it out after occupying it until November. There was a 20' x 40' cattle or machine shed along the road. In fact, it was right out in the road right-of-way! We moved that shed onto Lot 3 on a concrete slab. It was perfect! It became a garage and shop.

In the meantime, we paid $2,500 for a two-story house in downtown Naperville. We paid another $2,500 to have Herman Muehlfeldt and Sons move it to the farm which by now we were calling "Wheatland View."

Ernie Knight and his son Ernie were all-around tradesmen. They built block basement walls and remodeled the house. When we moved in late in November, our total cost came to $20,400. It was a very nice remodeled like-new home.

Meanwhile, Ed Webster was drawing tentative plats of the subdivision. It remained for us to accomplish the drainage, moving earth, and grading. Alan, Larry, Gordon, and I drove all over northern Illinois looking for machinery we could afford. What an education! Everything we found was too expensive.

Remember, we were learning how to farm, establishing the farmstead, starting a cattle herd, changing schools, selling real estate, and on and on—all at the same time! Finding suitable machinery for farming *and* earthmoving was an unending urgent need.

Matt Eipers, a farmer in what is now Bolingbrook, had a selling-out auction. A neighbor, Ed Fiene, went along with me to advise me. I bought an Allis Chalmers WD tractor with wide front and power steering, a

Farmall "B" tractor, an old wagon, a cultivator, and some other implements. I should have bought all of the machinery, but having spent over $2,000, I was afraid of Laurabelle's reaction. We had the valves ground on the WD, and later on, we bought a loader for it.

Gordon was about five years old when all of this action occurred. Larry was in eighth grade, and Alan was in high school. The three sons, Alan in particular, had responsibilities far beyond their years.

Meanwhile, the search for machinery continued. We had talked to dozens of implement dealers when we finally got a break! I stopped in again at Cromer Motors in Naperville. They were dealers of both autos and farm machinery. Bob, the head mechanic, asked, "Would you like to buy a tractor and earthmover all as one unit?" I cannot recall having been that excited in a long time.

Cromers had bid on a 1948 LAI Model Case tractor hooked to a 1948 LaPlante Choate all-hydraulic scraper. Cromer had failed to allow enough for the old machine and had lost the new tractor sale. The buyer was the Hillside Cemetery in Hillside, Illinois.

P and D of Des Plaines, Illinois, made the deal and took the old machine in trade. They had not yet picked it up, and Bob, the mechanic, knew about it. I got on the phone. P and D wanted quite a bit of money. I offered them $340 "as is," and they accepted my offer. I mailed a check and received a bill of sale.

At last we had our scraper. Now the fun began! The machine had not been run nor moved in several years. Three-inch diameter trees were growing through the frame. Five tires were flat, and the sixth was broken. No battery, the hood caving in and rusted, the gasoline line ruptured, no seat cushion, and wasps by the dozen.

We found the old girl parked in the fence row behind the cemetery maintenance building.

I called Robinson Tire and Auto store in Aurora, Illinois. They sent a tire repair unit, and I installed a repaired tire, inflated and checked the other five tires. Cost: $75.

The following Saturday, Alan and I were at that cemetery again. We oiled and greased everything. We cleaned the chrome rams with steel wool and gasoline and then smeared oil on them. The old girl was parked in the fence row behind the maintenance building.

We cut brush and trees off, under, and around the machine; then we hacked a path out of the bush. A long day's work!

A few days later, the local farm machinery repair genius and mechanic, Bruce Havens, and I went to the cemetery in his old Chevrolet panel service truck. "Shep," the old collie dog, was with us, of course. We removed the valve cover and "staked" the valves. Next, we removed, cleaned, rodded, and, after making a long gasket with 30 one-quarter inch holes, reassembled the cast iron tank radiator and bolted it back in place. About that time, the superintendent came walking out and gave us a battery and a seat cushion. We were getting closc!

I drove to Elmhurst in the truck to buy a gas line. Bruce tinkered with the "mag." The cemetery man gave us a piece of gutter down spout to use as an exhaust pipe. Finally, Bruce poured in some gas, and the moment of truth was at hand!

I climbed up, sat on the seat, pulled on the choke wire, stepped on the throttle with my left foot, pushed the starter button with the heel of my left hand, and suddenly...that old beauty was running! Soot flew, rust came off, and "zinged" from the fan and stuff. Shortly, it settled down and "ran like new." The hydraulic brakes worked, the clutch seemed perfect, and all of the gears meshed.

We wired down the gas tank and put on the "down spout exhaust pipe," "reefed" on the steering wheel, and we were ready to roll.

Our 1926 Model L tractor

I put her in first gear, engaged the clutch, and drove right out of the pile of brush, trees, and ruts. Free at last! Tied on a flag. Locked the gate. Headed for Naperville Farm Repair some 18 miles away. We stopped and bought ten gallons of gas.

As the miles rolled away, I got braver and opened her wide open. We were soon going 16 miles per hour. Incredible exhaust noise. The tractor had 440 cubic inches in a four-cylinder engine. Within an hour, we arrived at Bruce's repair shop.

The unit showed no signs of tender loving care. We added fenders, restored, or replaced some hoses. The steam-cleaning man charged $75 to blast off the worst of the baked-on accumulated grease-and-dirt mixture. Then we took the machine home where the whole family chipped, painted, scraped, and scraped to get it clean enough to paint. Ernie Knight, Jr., had a small air compressor and paint gun. He loaned it to us. It took eight gallons of paint applied one quart at a time. That was a long day!

Now, we had a very acceptable-looking and operating five-yard scraper. It would outwork many larger machines because it was fast and well-designed. It was also a marvelous grader.

Open bowl scrapers are designed to be push-loaded. One day Bruce said, "You need a push tractor. Clarence Landorf has a 1926 Model L tractor. He will take $115 for it." I went to Landorf's and brought it. The "L" was simple power at its best. It went about 1.5 miles per hour in first gear. We got more power and speed by increasing the rpms about 50 percent on all of our old Case tractors.

"Skin" Greenberg, Bruce's blacksmith partner, built a big push plate on the "L," and away we went. Now we could load six yards heaped in a minute or less, "nod" or "wave" off the pusher L, and stop and flip the LAI gear shift into third speed and move out to spread dump and return to the cut. We tried to make ten loads an hour. Most of the time, we did better than that. You could make a U-turn in 24 feet. It unloaded in seconds. It was built to last. We never had any structural failure.

The "L" ran on a magneto, of course. It had no generator system of any kind. It did not even have oil to the upper valve assembly. There was a plug in the top of the valve cover. Oiling the valves and rocker arms was accomplished by removing the plug and pouring in some oil every hour or so while operating. Worked fine. Soon, late fall was upon us again, and the days were shorter. Mel Royer, a good friend, arrived at 4:00 P.M. daily to drive the "L" pusher. He was soon highly skilled.

Faced with early twilight, we needed lights. Mel and I bolted two floodlights on the frame, built a box on the driver's platform, and ran a wire from a battery post directly to the lights. On the other cable, we installed a clamp. When Mel needed lights, he just reached down and clipped onto the other battery post. Juice consumption was of no concern because Mel needed lights only briefly as he came up behind me and made contact with the push block. I always knew where he was because I could see the flame of his exhaust pipe.

I was usually beginning to load by the time Mel caught me. Conversely, he knew when the pan was full by listening and feeling the increased rpm's as I raised the blade on the scraper and pulled away to change gears. The clutch and brake control consisted of a big lever. Back on the lever to go and forward to brake. The throttle was open all of the time.

One day Mel and I were cutting a steep bank in very hard, stony, yellow clay. Mel was on such a steep bank that some gas was leaking out through the vent of the gas cap. A certain amount of oil and gas always accumulated on the tractor. Suddenly, the spilled gas caught on fire. We had a BIG fire—at least a ten-foot flame. Mel could not get away because on a cut that steep, the brake would not hold. There was no ignition switch. The engine was shut off by reaching down by the starting crank to grab the choke and choke the engine to death. So, there he sat while I stopped, jumped over the fender, and grabbed the fire extinguisher.

After that incident, we soon installed an ignition switch. Ernie Knight; Ernie, Jr.; and Ken Strachen were working right near us. Strachen said, "Where else can you see a circus like that with no admission charge?"

––––––––––

Soon we located a 1939 Galion Model 101 road grader. Finally! Finally we could build and grade roads. We had come a long way!   ✳

My Car

To quote the venerable philosopher of the spinach can, "Once I was happy, but now I am forlorn…" and I am quickly becoming an old man. There was a time when I occasionally had a nickel in my pocket for as much as two full days, but today I roll into Haggarts and give my last nickel to Les, for that precious fluid that gives my pile of junk a new lease on life.

As I roar away, Les shouts his usual, "Hurry back!" and with a doleful look at the gas gauge, almost at the "zero" mark, I assure him that I will. The days I used to spend blissfully loafing and totally unaware of any of the disturbing elements around me are gone!

My car has most of the faults other cars have, and some faults peculiar to itself, which may no doubt be attributed to its being of a rare species, seldom seen but easily heard.

This lovely junk heap, which I profoundly curse at times, and, in still weaker moments, caress with a good swift kick in the dashboard, has a motor, a body, four fenders (if my brother has reformed), headlights, a taillight, and many other miscellaneous gadgets—some of which work, but the majority of which do not work—and in addition, four wheels.

Do you know what goes on those wheels? I'll tell you—tires! Have you ever bought a tire? Have you ever had a blowout and no spare tire? Have you ever patched a tube, put it in the tire, almost got it back on the rim, and then torn a hole in the tube with a tire iron? My friend, your education is yet to begin!

What? Sell my car to the junk man? Why, I'll have you know that that car is the best… Oh! You say you have ridden in it? Well, maybe I'd better…

❃

(Written on May 7, 1940, at the age of 17)

First Truck

In the first 24 years of our marriage, the subject of a truck often came up. I hauled stuff in the trunk. I built top carriers for our car. I bought and/or built trailers for our cars. I even paid people to haul stuff home from farm sales.

The answer to the idea of owning a truck was, "No, you don't need a truck!" Always!

Finally, one day I bought a 1957 Ford truck. I drove it home and parked it at the shed. Gordon and I started to work on it.

Not one word was ever spoken about the truck! That was one of the happiest and most important days of my life.

I intend to own a pickup truck as long as I live!

> I intend to own a pickup as long as I live!

"Are You Here to Get Your Instrument Rating?"

B ack—way back—in 1957, a group of local men and Mark and Jim, my brothers, built Aero Estates, an airport subdivision. We believe it was the first one ever built. A partnership built the residential subdivision and an associated partnership built and operated the airstrip.

Like many another young lad, I had long dreamed of becoming a pilot. At the onset of World War II, I tried to enlist in the United States Air Force, but I was refused because of having partial color blindness.

Then when suddenly I became involved in Aero Estates, I joined the Businessmen's Flying Club which operated from the strip which was then called Naper Aero.

The club owned a 1946 J3 Cub. An "old-pro" member, Arch Dewey, gave me a couple of orientation and primary lessons. Soon thereafter, I got Bill Blair, a United Airlines captain and neighbor, to be my personal instructor. I soloed at the old Wheatland-Matter Airstrip on a runway with a power line and 800 usable feet.

In the ensuing weeks, I went to ground school, flew, and clocked in several hours. Then I just became too busy with everyday affairs and quit flying.

> The story of my "back-to-school" experience to obtain my private pilot's license—at my age!

A number of years later, Wayne Miller, a longtime friend, came to me and said, "Say, why don't we buy an airplane and get our licenses?"

So we did! We bought a Piper Cherokee 180—a very nice airplane. Wayne based that plane at the Aurora Airport where he took instruction. That meant a drive of more than 30 minutes each way from our home. I just didn't do it.

Then along about 1975, our youngest son Gordon decided to become a pilot. By now, Wayne had lost interest and quit flying. I bought Wayne's share, and we based the airplane at Naper Aero after Gordon soloed.

Gordon hired a pilot to help him ferry the plane to Florida where he attended a flight school at Sebring and got his private license.

As I contemplated my age (along with the hoped-for likelihood of more free time), I decided to fly again and get a private pilot license. I attended ground school at the Aurora Airport, and my score on the written exam was passing.

About a year later, I called Flight Safety International at Vero Beach, Florida, and made arrangements to attend school there. Laurabelle and I took the motor home to Vero Beach. While there, we met a couple of men about my age who asked, "Are you here to get your instrument rating?" They, of course, were.

I laughingly told them, "No, I'm here to get my private pilot license." After only three weeks of instruction, the appointment was made for my check ride.

I waited around all day, and finally at 5:15 P.M., the examiner arrived. We took off, and all went well until we arrived at St. Lucie's Airport at dusk in the rain! The examiner instructed me to slip to a landing on Runway 36. I skidded toward the runway at which point the examiner asked, "Are you still landing on 36?"

"Yes," I replied.

He said, "You are lined up with 04."

"What should I do?" I asked.

"Go ahead and land on 04 and make it a soft field landing."

Nothing—absolutely nothing—went right from there on in, and I flunked the check ride.

I telephoned our son Gordon and told him I was coming home.

He said, "No! All that examiner wants now is to get rid of you. Stay there and take another check ride in a couple of days."

I did, and everything was absolute perfection. I finally had my license!

Lead Line

"Dad, it sounded like something hit that backstop with a 12-pound sledge hammer," said my son Gordon.

"It felt that way, too," said yours truly. We were talking about my head.

In 1979, we bought a beautiful Piper "Dakota." It had all the radios and instruments reasonably available. It "lived" in a rented hangar at Naper Aero Estates right near our home. Son Gordon is a professional pilot as far as training, ratings, and experience count.

Russ, Gordon, and I were pushing and pulling the airplane across patches of ice and snow into the hangar. Gordon had the tow bar hooked to the front wheels. Russ and I were pulling on a nylon lead line at the tail.

Thank you, Nikita!

Gordon said, "Let's go." We let go all right. The snaps on the nylon lead line broke, and I literally flipped backward and my head hit first!

I can still hear myself moaning, "I'm hurt. I'm hurt! Snow, snow, snow!"

They finally understood and packed the back of my head and neck in granular ice and snow. In a few minutes of time, my head cleared and I said, "Thank you, Nikita."

A few weeks later when my headache was gone, and I was relearning telephone numbers that had been wiped out, I asked Gordon, "Did you hear me say, 'Thank you, Nikita' while I was lying on the ice?"

Gordon said, "No, I didn't."

Well, I guess I said it to myself, for you see, I was wearing a heavy, thick Astrakhan fur hat. It saved my skull. "Thank you, Nikita!"   ❉

D-X Station Truck Stop
Hayer and Springborn

In the mid-30's, Bill Hayer and Henry Springborn had been operating a successful gas station on Aurora Avenue and Eagle Street in Naperville. With the coming of Route 34 around the north part of town, the truck traffic would soon virtually disappear from their area. Then the cattle trucks and freight trucks going right up Washington Street would be north of town on the new Ogden Avenue.

Bill and Henry bought a whole block of frontage on the new highway. It consisted of the south side of Ogden from Loomis to Sleight Streets. The service station and gas pumps were located on the Loomis Street side of the Pine Knot Restaurant; parking lots occupied the east side. The big "D-X" logo of Midwest Petroleum as much in evidence. The whole establishment was "state-of-the-art" for that time. Six gas pumps, general repair and tire repair bays, a hydraulic hoist bay, a pit bay, big overhead doors, washrooms, a large work bench, and about 30 bunks were available to truckers at no charge.

The Pine Knot Restaurant was completely finished with knotty-pine board paneling. It seated about 50 patrons.

Bert Wilson and his wife were the first tenant operators. In those days, they fried everything. You could smell beef tallow and lard a block away. The place was wonderfully busy 24 hours a day. The staff of waitresses included some well-known Naperville girls.

Sunday night was the busiest evening of the week; 30 or 40 cattle trucks lined up as gasoline and/or restaurant patrons. Unbelievable! Four hours later, the truckers again stopped on the return trip from the Chicago Stockyards on the way to their next load of cattle from farms across the corn belt. Truckers patronizing the D-X Truck Stop served farms within 70 or 80 miles of the stockyards.

During the fall of 1940, I foolishly decided that I could attend college and also pump gas at the D-X station. "Foolish" is right. Thirty-five cents an hour was not fair—especially when working on the 3:00 to 11:00 P.M. shift. We worked extremely hard—shoveled snow, repaired tires, greased cars and trucks, washed cars and trucks, and kept the station scrubbed clean.

As he drove away, he began to laugh.

I contracted pneumonia and almost died. When I recovered, I returned to school and work, but not for long. I quit—just barely! Here's how I quit my job.

We had no cash register or cash drawer or even a strongbox. We just used a folded tally sheet on the counter. We carried all the money in our pockets. We made change wherever we were—indoors, outdoors, wherever.

On a blustery, rainy, cold night, one more customer drove up to Pump 3 and said, "One dollar," the most common gas purchase. I put in the gas, stepped to the driver's door, and gave him nine dollars in change for his ten-dollar bill.

As he drove away, he started to laugh uproariously. I did not realize why he was laughing until we counted the money from my shift. That's right! I had given him change for a ten-dollar bill. Only one thing was wrong—he had only given me a folded single in the darkness and rain!. I believe I would recognize that guy if I saw him today!

When Hank Springborn saw the shortage, he told a fellow employee of long service that he was going to fire me. When I came in at 3:00, Al told me I was going to be fired. I got back into my car and drove straight to the old station downtown where Bill Hayer ran the office and quit! Bill Hayer said, "All right, Johnny," and paid what wages were due me.

The next day, I went to work for the Lee Nelson Pure Oil Station at more money per hour, with no truck tire repairs, good lights, and off work at 9:00 P.M.

Should have gotten short-changed sooner!   ✸

What If I Could...

Go out the walk to the driveway, get into my 1933 Plymouth sport coupe and just go! That's right, just go! Given my desperate desire to be free and independent, the ownership of a car went a long way to fulfilling that desire.

My brother Bob and I bought a 1927 Hupmobile in 1938. It was a fine old car in near-mint condition. The tires were shot, and 20-inch used tires were hard to find. Bob had an accident with it; we couldn't afford to fix it, so we sold it.

In 1940, I bought a 1931 Ford Model A coupe for $32.50. It needed paint, two tires, and a valve job. It got them. However, I was hospitalized with pneumonia, and I sold the car to pay my hospital bill. Once again, I felt terribly frustrated.

Now we are back to the point of it all—my third car. A local fellow had a good 1933 Plymouth coupe. All it needed was paint and tires. I bought it for $65. My friend "Ky" Brand and I sanded it down. Brummels' Buick garage painted it black with red wheels. It was a really sharp little car. It had a radio, a heater, and a defroster fan. No muffler, just a straight pipe. (Guess what! That was the car that Brand and I drove to Plymouth, Michigan, at Thanksgiving time in 1942 where I met Laurabelle!)

My passion to be free to go places or to just roam was not really a good thing. Too often I walked down the back walk, cut classes, and just went driving.

Today, as I look back, it is obvious that I could never own and operate a car, attend college classes, and work 40 hours a week pumping gas and repairing truck tires. School suffered.

I tried to join the Air Corps. I had less than perfect color perception—"color blind."

The various "V" programs offered to college students were an obvious scam. The records show that I withdrew from North Central College. Frankly, when the draft was instituted, I just stopped attending class for the most part. Through it all, my mother paid my tuition at N.C.C. How? I will never know how she did it.

So…down the back walk to the car. Freedom to work…but the price of that freedom was too dear!

Too soon the letter came. "Greetings from the President of the United States…" I was drafted.

The car battery was removed and sat in the corner of the laundry room. The car was jacked up and rested on wood log blocks. An old tarp covered the front end. The antifreeze was drained, and mothballs were sprinkled inside the car to discourage rodents.

Every time my mother looked out of the kitchen window, there was the car. Mother mounted a campaign. Tear-stained letters, argumentative pleas, a persistent buyer, on and on. I relented, and she sold the car for $35. What a terrible mistake, for as it turned out, I needed that car!

I entered the U.S. Army at Fort Sheridan, Illinois, on February 3, 1943. The following day we shipped out to Camp Grant. In March, I was promoted to T/5 and went to Fort Benjamin Harrison at Indianapolis, Indiana, to attend dental technical school.

Boy, how I could have used that car! We got weekend passes from 4:00 P.M. Friday until 7:00 P.M. Monday. It was only 150 miles from Fort Harrison to Naperville and about 300 miles to Plymouth, Michigan, where Laurabelle's folks lived. Laurabelle often spent the weekend in Plymouth, for she taught school in Dryden, a little town about an hour's drive from Plymouth.

When I returned from service in December 1945, there was "my" sharp little 1933 Plymouth car running around Naperville! In retrospect, I should have rented a garage somewhere in town to store the car while I was in the service. Hopefully, my mother would not have hounded me into selling the car—"out of sight, out of mind."   ✳

Thresherman's Water Wagon

This *circa* 1840 thresherman's water tank is a rare survivor of the heyday of steam power across the American farm scene. Steam power reigned from before the Civil War until after World War I.

It may well be that this wagon was serviced and/or repaired in the Fry blacksmith shop on the old Fry homestead on Naperville-Plainfield Road.

The typical custom thresherman's outfit consisted of a steam traction engine and a threshing machine commonly referred to as a separator. The balance of the train of equipment depended upon the nature of the chore of the next farmer employing the thresherman's services. Basically, the chores consisted of grain threshing, clover hauling, and hay pressing.

Typically, the basic equipment consisted of a water wagon, a wood/coal/slabs wagon, and a plank wagon for strengthening and overlaying bridges as encountered. The water wagon was most important. The units of the assembly were often pulled as a train with the steam traction engine serving as motive power.

The thresherman usually carried an extra long wagon pole on each wagon so that teams of horses could be used for long hauls or in bad road conditions.

Gasoline or kerosene-fueled tractors rapidly became available and proved much "handier" and far less cumbersome. Soon the thrilling chug and huff of the steam engine drifted out of hearing as the wind and the wail of the whistle faded away in the distance. ❉

My 1933 Plymouth

In the late summer of 1941, I bought my third car. I have owned about 40 cars and trucks. Can I name a favorite? You bet your life! First, I had a 1927 Hupmobile in mint condition.

Next I had refurbished a 1930 Ford Model A coupe. It cost me $32.50. I spent an additional $10 for a valve job, $25 for a gun-metal gray paint job, $32 for tires and some miscellaneous hands-on things. It was a nice car.

Just about the time it was in perfect condition, I sold it for $140 to a Mr. George Cole. He gave it to his hired man on his farm in Indiana. At the time I sold it, I was a patient with pneumonia in St. Charles Hospital. The $140 was the amount of my hospital bill. Now I was without a car.

The moral? Don't always do as your mother asks!

In 1933, Chrysler had built a Plymouth coupe with a rumble seat. A fellow who frequented the service station where I worked knew of such a car for sale. I went to his home to see the car. It was a dandy little car, but it had fallen on hard times and was kind of a mess. The fellow who had owned it had driven it hard, but it still ran perfectly. I paid $65 for the car "as is."

The tires were shot. No muffler. A bad rear spring. It needed a paint job; it had been painted with a brush, and very sloppily done. Fiberboard interior trim panels for doors and the rumble seat. Some moldings gone—much more.

At the time, I was working part time at the Lee Nelson Pure Oil Station. One of the advantages of working in a service station was that we could buy items and parts at lower or discounted prices. Also, our working hours were flexible. Vic Jorgensen and I arranged our schedules so that Lee Nelson, the owner, rarely had to work evenings.

Years before, I had hand-sanded cars for Bernie Brummel, the body man at Brummel Buick. He agreed to paint the Plymouth for $25 if I sanded it. "Ky" Brand, a close friend and fellow tenor in the North Central College octette, helped with the sanding. We sanded for a couple of days and then sanded some more. Shortly, I had a slick black coupe with red wheels!

I learned that the engine had been overhauled, and the clutch and transmission had been rebuilt just before I bought it. I visited a junkyard where they had a "twin" to my car, and I got many miscellaneous items there. I still did not have any good tires, but I was an expert tire repairman. I really used a bunch of boots. Tires like those will hold up pretty well in cold weather, but in hot weather, they just blow out. Good enough for now.

Within a few weeks, it was a very nice car! My total investment was finally about $120. It was a good car—mechanically as well as…uh…cute! It cruised at about 55 miles per hour. It had a radio. A small rubber-bladed defroster fan was mounted on the dashboard. The single wiper was on the driver's side, of course, and slowed down and speeded up as the engine rpms affected the intake manifold pressure. No muffler. Just a noisy straight pipe. So actually, it only needed a right rear spring and a muffler to be "up in shape."

However, the little Plymouth was going on a big trip with neither the spring nor the muffler. A straight pipe ran all the way from the exhaust to the rear bumper. It wasn't too noisy in the car, but the world out there could hear it "loud and clear."

Shortly before Thanksgiving, Ky Brand called and asked if he could borrow the Plymouth to drive to Plymouth, Michigan. His fiancee, Betty Reidt, was spending Thanksgiving with a teacher associate at her family home in Plymouth, a small town about 30 miles southwest of Detroit. More importantly, the drive to Plymouth was 300 miles.

I told Ky, "No! You can't take the car. If you have trouble when you are alone, you wouldn't know what to do. However, I am willing to go with you." So, that's how it was.

Along about 9:30 or 10:00 P.M., Ky and I took off for Michigan. The little car ran flawlessly. We arrived at Plymouth at dawn. When we knocked on the door, a Mr. Wileden chased us away and told us to come back later. This was the weekend when Laurabelle and I first met.

On Sunday night after Thanksgiving, Ky and I took off for home. Sixty miles down the road in Jackson, Michigan, we stopped at an intersection. Ky popped the clutch. Bang—one broken spring. The man in the service station on the corner was just closing and had already turned off the gas pump lights.

Really nice guy! He helped us get the Plymouth on the hoist. All the remaining leaves of the right rear spring had snapped off just ahead of the axle. That meant we had proper alignment but no suspension.

We cut some pieces of 2 x 4 boards, bolted them to the frame, and lowered the car onto the 2 x 4's. It worked just fine, but can you imagine how it rode? The tires took all of the shock of everything on the road, and that was it. No spring or shock absorber suspension! Two hundred forty miles at 30 miles per hour! Sheer murder!

Laurabelle

It still was a wonderful trip. Ky saw Betty, and I got pretty well acquainted with Laurabelle Wileden. That's right! Our trip was the beginning of it all.

Laurabelle and I corresponded frequently, and soon made plans for Christmas.

On February 1, 1943, I parked the Plymouth in the back yard. I jacked it up and put logs under the corners of the frame. The battery was removed and stored in the summer kitchen room on our old home on Spring Avenue. Then I sprinkled it full of mothballs, covered it with some old tarps, and left for the Army.

It all sounds so simple that I can't believe yet how unhappily things turned out. Every time my mother looked out the kitchen window, she saw that car! She nagged me unceasingly about selling that car. She wanted me to sell it, and she told me so. (Too bad I couldn't have found a garage in which to store the car.)

After a few tear-besmirched letters, enough was enough, and I finally wrote, "Sell the car." She did. She practically gave it away—for $35.

One of the worst times of my life! Later I was stationed at Fort Harrison in Indianapolis and then at Camp Ellis, Illinois. Oh, how Laurabelle and I could have used that car!

When I returned from the war just short of three years later and visited Naperville, there was the '33 Plymouth running merrily down Spring Avenue. When I returned from Michigan two years later, there was the '33 Plymouth still running down Spring Avenue. When did it finally end? The guy moved to Wisconsin!

The moral? Don't always do as your mother asks! In the Henry Ford Museum at Greenfield Village, a 1933 Plymouth like mine is parked right up by the front of the parade of automobiles. When I stop to look at it, I am not happy!   ✼

The Zephyr

In 1932, I was a student in the fifth grade at Ellsworth School. The Chicago World's Fair, "The Century of Progress" was in full swing.

Since before the Civil War, steam had been the motive choice for power. There were, of course, some electric rail lines. They drew current from a third rail or overhead cables which, in turn, powered electric motors between the axle trucks. Now, however, we were about to see the first streamlined, unitized, standard steel, high-speed passenger train—the Zephyr.

The Zephyr was powered by a diesel-electric locomotive. A diesel engine powered a generator which, in turn, furnished electricity to electric motors right down at the level of axle-spring truck assemblies. Efficient, clean, reasonably economical, and required much less maintenance than a steam engine.

Now the time had come for the inaugural Denver to Chicago run— non-stop! Mechanical trouble almost delayed the run, but somehow the problems were solved. Word came to the local train station by telegraph that the Zephyr was on her way. As school children, we marched the three blocks over to the railroad tracks and waited. Most of the town was there.

At last, a flicker of reflected sunlight, the distant wail of the big electric horn, and sure enough, down the track came the streaking, silver Zephyr. She slowed all the way through town, and we cheered madly.

Little did we think or even dream that in a few years the tens of thousands of steam engines across the country would be gone. The rumbling diesel electric engines would take their places!

I am told that the Republic of China is the only remaining builder of railway steam engines. I never cease to marvel when people talk of off-the-shelf components and build something like the diesel electric-powered locomotive Zephyr. What next?   ❊

Second Gear, Gordie

In the winter of 1961, a neighboring farmer, Ed Fiene, and I attended the Matt Eipers closing-out action. I bought a 1951 IHC tractor with a wide front and power steering. Also a 1947 Farmall "B" tractor, a two-row cultivator, an old hayrack, a three-bottom IHC mounted plow, and some miscellaneous items. (I should have bought more, but I did not realize that until later.)

The big news, however, was the Allis Chalmers (AC) tractor with wide front and power steering. Gordon ("Gordie" in those days) fell in love with the tractor, and, by age eight or nine, it sort of became Gordie's tractor. It had a four-speed transmission: first gear—1½ miles per hour; second gear—3 miles per hour; third gear—7 miles per hour; and fourth gear—12 miles per hour. Gordie was limited to second gear. As he grew and gained experience, he was allowed to progress to third gear and finally to the fourth gear.

When it was obvious that Gordie was in third gear rather than second, someone always would meet him and say, "Second gear Gordie."

In time, Gordon became and is now a masterful machine operator, farmer, and airplane pilot with hands-on experience as repairman, rebuilder, operator, and owner of a whole galaxy of machines.

Specifically, Gordon is a wonderful airplane pilot as well as an experienced and very capable real estate development superintendent. After all, his experience and acquired skills go all the way back to "Second gear Gordie!"

❋

The Old Fox

Back in 1924, the Naperville city fathers bought a new Ahrens-Fox fire truck. It was a dandy. Rear-wheel brakes were operated by a lever worked by the engineer or fireman in the right seat-—huge pressure dome mounted up front, big chrome hand-operated bell—low, dignified siren also worked by the man in the right seat—fold-down windshield.

This big pumper was painted red, of course, and lavishly trimmed in gold lettering and fleur-de-lis. The tires were enameled in black. The whole machine exuded power and romance. Everything from the ladder to the hand suction pump, to the racked nozzles, either sparkled or gleamed.

What a glorious way to save herself from retirement!

But best of all were the sounds. The great six-cylinder engine murmured and clicked as it fired and ran. The exposed overhead valve train tapped—all combining to send a great roar of pure power out of the three-inch "beller" pipe at the rear of the truck. The exhaust pipe noise was such that the engine actually made as much or more noise than the low-voiced, slow-moaning siren.

When it pulled out of the firehouse downtown, the rumble of the engine could be heard for several blocks in all directions.

Of course, it was called a pumper, and so it was. It is said that even today the Old Fox can pump more water than any other engine in the Naperville Fire Department.

The Old Fox fought the Aurora S. S. Kresge fire, the Owen Kane Ford fire, the Nichols Gym fire, the Old Main Fire, the Methodist Church fire, and hundreds of miscellaneous conflagrations.

Farm fires were probably the most frustrating. Due to the response time and the limited water available, fires in barns were usually heavily involved by the time the engines arrived.

For now, the Old Fox is in operating condition and stands waiting for the call. Sounds unlikely? It is.

However, in 1951 I believe, a child playing with matches and candles set a fire in the Methodist church, one of the largest structures in town. The volunteer firefighters arrived in a timely manner. They pulled up to the hydrant on the corner with their new engine, connected the hard suction hose, spun all of the fancy valves, but guess what? No pressure. Firemen Fred Galow and Wendell Flory were at the end of the upstairs hall at the heart of the fire calling, "Pressure!" Once again, no pressure. The Fire Protection District truck was now on line with its moderate pumping capacity. Nearby communities had dispatched help, but the fire was now out of control.

In the midst of the panic and frustration could be heard the deep-throated wail and the powerful rumble of the Ahrens Fox as it pulled up to Franklin Street and rolled right up to the hydrant at Washington Street. Now what? No hose. No ladders, no suction hose. Plenty of dust and miscellaneous debris. But most of all, a heart that was true. What a glorious way to save herself from retirement!

Hastily hooked up with shared and borrowed equipment, the Fox came on line with a light tattoo, then with a measured beat and finally with a vibrating, wheel-blocked, put-out-the-fire, full-throated roar. What a sight! Doyle Steck, the off-duty engineer who drove the Fox to the fire, reached up to the big throttle lever and pushed it past full throttle. The Fox leaped to respond. Now a veritable flood of water was hitting the inferno in the church wing. It took four men to hold each nozzle and hose.

Hours passed, and the flames were gradually snuffed out and dampened. The fire is under control.

The cleanup begins. Now the Old Fox rests. Low on white-gas fuel, an oil leak here and there, crackling and sighing as the heavy iron engine begins to cool. A little steam escapes the jacket. Doyle Steck, still in street clothes, hovers over the wonderful machine—oil can in one hand and cotton shop towel in the other.

Retire the Fox?   ✳

Faces of Friendship

If a man does not make new acquaintances
as he advances through life,
he will soon find himself oft alone;
one should keep his friendships
in constant repair.
–Samuel Johnson

Barney

It's a raw, windy, freezing day in February. As I stand hunched against the wind with the ear flaps of my hunting cap pulled down, I wait for the auction to start.

Farm sale here today. Muddy and freezing underfoot. Farmers' pickups and cars string the road for a half mile or so. Probably 200 farmers. Almost all men. A lunch wagon truck lurches in and plugs into an electric outlet on the yard light pole.

The auction wagon truck pulls in behind. The first items of "stuff" are referred to as "rack items." Comes the shout from the auctioneer, "All right! We're gonna start the sale! Terms are cash or check before you move anything. Hullo, Pat! You doing the clerking? Good! All right, what's the first item?"

At this point, two men climb onto the hay wagon. Given a moment, they move aside some items, avoid some rotten boards, and find a place to stand.

There I stood— crying in the rain.

I, like many others, was not at the sale to buy anything. I went to talk to folks, and, at an opportune moment, to talk to a real estate broker who had buyers for certain lands. The weather was not helping any. It was only 25°, and the gathering was now getting more sleet and snow.

I was hunched in the corner of a shed, talking to some friends when I noticed Barney coming toward me. Barney was a retired farmer and a tough Prussian who spoke loudly. He may have been a cavalry officer in World War I. Since the death of his lovely wife, he had changed drastically. He dressed casually. He had become a heavy drinker. Some things just don't change though—he had a heavy accent and loud voice. However, his sharp eyes and quick wit made me realize that he was an excellent grammarian and still a brilliant man.

Now, as I stood alone for a moment, here comes Barney walking toward me. He was red in the face and puffing a little from his tough walk across the barnyard. He was dressed for the weather—heavy wool trousers, felt boots partly laced, wool flannel shirt, long underwear showing, a dress tie neatly dividing the open shirt neck, a heavy corduroy cap with ear muffs tied down, and ear flaps askew. Add to all of that, a heavy canvas hunting coat and double-thumbed orange gloves, and you have a warm old cavalryman, trained engineer, farmer, and widower.

He is lonely! Lurching a little as he came across the rough, now beginning-to-freeze ground, he came to a halt inches from my face. He took a deep breath, and, with a winning vehemence said, "Frèu (Fry), it doesn't make a bit of difference how many mistakes you make in raising those boys as long as you imbue them with knowledge that you are doing the best you know how and tell them that you *luff* (love) them."

Now, there I stood! How did Barney know that I, his 44-year-old friend, needed to hear *his* words of wisdom? There I stood—crying in the rain. ✽

The Bread Man

The Bread Man drove his big old green purveyor truck into our lives long about 1935 as he parked at the corner of Loomis and Sixth Streets right by Rechenmacher's house.

This genial older fellow dealt in day-old and stale bread. He had all kinds of bread, rolls, buns, coffeecakes, and cakes in various stages of staleness or comparative freshness.

We had a supply of burlap bags or gunny sacks. For 25 cents, he would fairly well fill a bag with stuff to be used as chicken and rabbit feed. For 50 cents a bag, the better quality stuff was good enough that we could use a lot of it.

We were especially fond of the Parker House rolls. After removing the waxed paper wrapping, we sprinkled them with water and heated them in the oven. Five boys could go through a dozen rolls in a hurry!

Five boys could go through a dozen rolls in a hurry!

The Bread Man usually came on Wednesday evenings. We kids really looked forward to his coming.

One Wednesday he did not appear. We never saw him again—but I remember him. �֍

Eldie (L.D.) Lambert

It was the industrial hub of the town of Naperville. Emblazoned on everything they owned was the legend, "Kroehler Mfg. Co.—World's Largest Maker of Upholstered Furniture." More than 600 men and women were employed at "The Shack" in Naperville.

As makers and sellers of tens of thousands of pieces, a fleet of trucks was needed at each of their plants. Eldie Lambert was the man who made the trucks go at the Naperville plant.

We lived just two blocks away and passed the Kroehler garage going to and from school. The large, red-brick garage was near the corner of Loomis and Fifth Avenue. It was four stalls wide, and there were chain-operated, corrugated-steel doors on the four stalls.

He did lose his patience with me— one time.

In the early 1930's, the standard trucks at Kroehler were long-type, Buick straight trucks. They were about 40 feet long and had a tailgate with canvas curtains at the back. These were single-axle trucks. Eight-cylinder, overhead valve, in-line gasoline engines gave them considerable power. Furniture is bulky rather than heavy, so the trucks with four speeds performed quite well. The Kroehler trucks were all painted light-green with letters in dark green and gold. In later years, the trucks were painted dark green.

There were several Kroehler plants in places such as Binghamton, New York; Kankakee, Illinois; Canada; California; and North Carolina, to name a few places. The most frequent runs were to the colossal structure in Chicago called the "Furniture Mart," or just "The Mart."

In the early thirties, there were about ten of the big trucks in Naperville, and one small straight body truck used for local work.

The big garage near the corner of Loomis and Fifth Avenue was Eldie Lambert's domain. With one part-time helper, he maintained that fleet of trucks. What a wonderful domain! As "the fixer" at our house, I was magically welcome at the Kroehler garage. The floor shone. The tools gleamed. The Pure Oil gasoline pump was clean and dry.

This was where we checked our bike tires. This was where we sat on a bench and listened to Eldie talk. This was where we watched them change and repair tires. I don't even remember them swearing much. How odd!

As trucks returned from their runs, they were washed, all levels checked, and the tires carefully checked. Those were still the days of the cotton-ply, high-pressure tires. Most larger tires were 7.50 x 20. Tire rims had the now-outlawed locking rings. Later rims, as with rims and wheels today, are not inclined to "blow" and kill people. However, I have fixed thousands of tires, and I never met one I could trust!

Eldie was patient with "us kids." Lost valve caps and cores were ours for the picking up if they were outside the garage doors. He also had cold water to drink. Sometimes I spent the day just watching him and asking questions. He did lose patience with me one time. The International truck suffered a burnt valve right at the time of the annual Furniture Mart Show. The valve had to be ground—RIGHT NOW! I was all eyes and ears. I was standing as close as I could get and absolutely chattering questions. Suddenly, Eldie raised his voice to a near shout. I am glad that I have finally forgotten his exact words—"Johnny, get out of the way and be quiet!" I think it was harsher than that and included sending me home.

A couple of weeks later, I returned. Nothing was ever said. In those days, "men" could not fix things like that very well. They didn't say, "I'm sorry."

Now, in a lighter vein! Eldie bought a three-wheeled motorcycle made from two machines. For some reason, it was built with reversed directions. In other words, if you wanted to go left, you turned right! It had incredible power—he wrecked it!

I cannot begin to share how much I learned from listening to Eldie and to his cronies who stopped by. They never lacked for ideas.

Some time later, we moved to the other side of town. I did not see Eldie Lambert much after that move, but I have never forgotten him!   ✹

"Ves" Neville

He stood tall—a man of dignity and strength.
—gentle without being weak
—kindly in speech
—accepting everybody as they were
—loving God and His church
—secure, even in his human imperfections
—a constant husband and father
—a good example
—a man of courage
—expressing freely the music in his soul
—living long in memory

He was, most of all, *a good man*!

Lowell White

The Great Depression had the world in its terrible grip. In the male work force, unemployment ran about 40 percent. It was 1934. There was no economic health in sight. Local governments floundered. Churches were not organized or so moved to be of continuing down-to-earth help. Things were bad.

About that time, a young man came to town as minister of the Brethren Church. He and his family moved into the newly remodeled parsonage next door to the church at 119 W. Benton Avenue. His name was Ralph White. The former Virginian became a person of real influence to the town. Reverend White was the first chairman or president of both the Naperville Council of Churches and the Naperville's Ministers' Association.

By whatever means, Naperville was apprized of funds and put into place the Federal Works Progress Administration (WPA). One of the "benefits" of the WPA was the plan to convert an abandoned quarry into a very large outdoor swimming pool, promptly named "Centennial Beach." In the local lexicon, it became "The Beach," and so it stands.

I believe "The Beach" opened in 1934. It promptly became a Mecca for most families. People came from miles around for "The Beach" had a capacity of about 3,000 people. Naperville was the envy of many other towns in northeastern Illinois. Almost everyone applauded "The Beach."

During the thirties, the dreaded disease of poliomyelitis (polio) was a crippler or even a killer of thousands of people. Many people, my parents among them, tried to keep their children away from "The Beach." They said that the infusion of daily chlorine and of fresh water was inadequate. They were partially right. Aside from polio, it was obvious that minor scratches and cuts became infected.

The White family lived only a few blocks from "The Beach." Their son Lowell, who was nearly a teenager, almost lived at "The Beach." He fell prey to what I now suppose was some kind of staph infection. He developed a cyst on his spine, and the result was complete paralysis from the waist down. When he became a paraplegic, many blamed "The Beach."

Now, here is Lowell White, a wheelchair user at the age of 12. How will he get to and from school? When he arrived, who will hold the doors? How about the stairs? No ramps in those days. The answers soon came.

Wade Matheray lived at 230 W. Spring Avenue, just two blocks to the west of the high school building. He was a strong guy. I don't know why, but he was being reared by his grandparents. Wade sort of adopted Lowell and his wheelchair.

To get to the parsonage at 119 W. Benton Avenue, Wade went out the back door to the alley, and then back down the alley and then a block and a half to Benton Ave. There, he loaded Lowell, his sanitary supplies, a lap robe, a raincoat, and a cap. These items, together with his lunch, rode in a wire basket on the back of the wheelchair. Off to school!

There were two routes of about equal length. It depended on who was going to help with Lowell. Most often, I think they went up the hill to Washington Street and then north to the school. The big, high-wheeled chair navigated street curbs fairly well. Stairways were something else. Just picture this.

Here comes Lowell—streaking down the halls in his chair. When he arrived at the stairs, four guys would grab the carrying handle, and up the stairs they would go. Lowell, of course, was wonderfully strong from the waist up. His arms and hands were like spring steel.

Well, you say, we have seen folks in wheelchairs before. What's so special?

It's Wade! Yes, it's Wade. It's the guys who carried Lowell.

Let's see, how does it go? How does it go? Oh, yes! *And the King shall answer and say unto them, Verily I say unto you, Inasmuch as ye have done it unto one of the least of these my brethren, ye have done it unto me."* (Matthew 25:40)

❋

Wally Boughton

The following is a letter I wrote to Wally during the Christmas 1991 holiday season.

Dear Wally,

I remember when about 30 years ago you bought Bill Kohley's truck and began hauling stone. You came to me twice and asked if you could furnish the stone for our first little section of road in Wheatland View. I explained to you that we were already committed to a deal with "Augie" Ritzert. I was not free to tell you that Augie was carrying us until we sold some lots.

See you along the trail, Wally.

The years went by, and you eventually got your own pit—the same one from which my great-grandfather and my grandfather had hauled when they built many of our township roads. Not long afterward, I received a phone call from your dad, Walter Boughton, Sr. He said, "John, I think it's time to sell. I don't know you very well, but I think you have good partners."

We met and talked about price, exchanges, and time table. As we parted, he said, "I'll call you Thursday night." He called as promised. Bob Carr and I met with him, worked out the details, and shook hands. I don't think we ever had a contract.

To make a long story short, the farms were exchanged and monies paid as asked and directed. Everyone moved. Wally stayed on a few months while he and Carol built their new home. The whole deal worked like a charm!

We finished up Shell Lake and began work at your folks' farm which, by that time, we had named Wheatland South. I told you, "Any time your truck is available, bring stone." From day to day, we marked a plat so Van knew where to haul. Some days Van brought only a load or two, but sometimes he brought 24 loads. Partner Bob Carr audited the tickets and delivered our check. It worked swell! As the years passed, we always had Boughton trucks taking care of us. What a happy relationship!

- Wally, you have always been good to talk to.
- You always recognized my voice when I called.
- Not many people can tell a story better than you can.
- You have always been a man of your word.
- You too have worked with your sons—not always easy.
- I wonder if you have sometimes wondered, as I have, about the "right-ness" of decisions past.
- People always think of you as a strong man.
- When we need help from you as an investor, you are a tremendous help.

The time came when you began to experience symptoms of impending illness. From that time until now, I have been inspired by your positive attitude and indomitable spirit. I thank God every single day for that.

I say to Him, "It will be wonderful if Wally can return to vigorous good health." Again and again, I ask, "Help Wally continue his marvelous attitude and courageous outlook."

At times when we parted, you would say, "See you along the trail." I do not know if you ever realize how much that farewell means to people. I treasure it as one more memory.

"See you along the trail, Wally!"   ✽

The Faithfulness of Family

The family is one of nature's masterpieces.
–George Santayana

Bessie and Ren's Wedding—
"Come High Water!"

April 5, 1947—a day to remember. Not, however, just for the wedding.

I was attending college after getting out of the Army. We had a "hole-in-the-wall" apartment in Willow Run. It was a World War II temporary housing camp built for the Willow Run bomber plant at nearby Ypsilanti, Michigan.

Now, just after the war, it was tenanted by college students and other folks on various kinds of public aid or still serving at war plants as industrial plants in the greater Detroit area were switching from wartime to peacetime economy. Lousy place! Huge roaches!

Laurabelle's folks lived about 12 miles east at Plymouth, Michigan. Our first child was due about the end of May, so Laurabelle was very pregnant!

This was Laurabelle's sister Bessie's wedding day. She had met Reynold "Ren" Dodds some months before. Her father, Alfred Wileden, said he thought they would "hitch up" all right.

Ren and Bessie

The plans were all set for a formal wedding at the home of the bride. A reception and buffet would follow. A large crowd was expected.

The Saturday morning of the wedding day finally arrived. It appeared to be a normal, late spring day.

Our 1937 Plymouth coupe started and ran well. Away we went. We realized it had rained most of the night, but we had no idea how much it had rained up the river just a short way.

Route 12, Old Michigan Boulevard, ran from Detroit west. The land in southeast Michigan is only a few feet above Lake Erie water level. Sewage and storm waters have to be pumped. All of this is by way of introducing the worst flood we had ever seen. As we turned onto Route 12, the pavement was covered with running water and manhole covers were askew. Uh-oh! We faced five miles on Route 12, and then five miles north on Ford Road.

Quicker than I can tell it, the floorboards were under water, and the engine was beginning to run rough. Laurabelle had long since sort of curled up with her feet off of the floor. Our "going-to-a-wedding" clothes were *safe* in the trunk of our car.

By now, the highway was littered with drowned-out autos, trucks, and buses. The mess called for immediate action! Minutes later, we realized that the creek was also rising!

Quicker than I can tell it, the floorboards were under water...

I shut off the engine, removed my shoes and socks, rolled up my pants legs, folded back the hood side panels, and got my tool box from the trunk.

The distributor, coil, and plugs were only about four inches out of the water. However, by now, the fan blades were about six inches *in* the water. Only one thing to do—remove the fan belt, start the engine, and idle forward in first gear. It was imperative that we make no wave or wash. It all depended on how I steered the automobile for the remembered high spots of road lane and/or shoulder. Didn't have to worry about the wake from other cars and vehicles—they were all drowned out!

Now the questions plaguing my mind were: Will the engine overheat without a fan? Can we keep the distributor out of the water? We crept along for about four miles, and eventually we reached the intersection of Ford Road and our Route 12.

By now, the engine was boiling, and the generator was steaming a little. We stopped. We waited until the engine coolant stopped boiling. I reinstalled the fan belt and let the engine cool down.

Laurabelle and I thought we had it made now. But the worst was yet to come! We turned north on Ford Road. The rain had stopped. Still no traffic, of course, and the old Plymouth was running like new!

Now as we approached the Ecorse intersection, it appeared impossible for us to continue. The river bridge just beyond the intersection was flooded at least six inches too deep to traverse. Stalled cars had water at least six inches above the floorboards. "Now what?"

From what I can remember, while we had to go about 100 yards through the water, there was only a short section of road where the water would drown out the engine. I decided to try. Up came the side panels, off came the fan belt again, and we were ready. I backed up a ways. Here we go!

"If we can hit the deep spot fast enough, I think we can get to higher ground before we drown out." *Wide open in first. Wide open in second.* "Hang on, honey!"

By the time we hit the deepest water, we were making about a two-foot wave right up over the front fender and into the engine. Amidst a cloud of steam, we slowed. I kicked in the clutch and held down the accelerator. The engine fell off to three cylinders, then to two cylinders, then sat there banging and shaking as a third cylinder gradually came in. A fourth began hitting now and then, and I *knew* we could make it.

So, hitting on four of six, we crept along. Then disaster almost struck. Some dummy in a pickup truck came sailing at us, passed beside us, and drowned out.

This was almost too much for the old Plymouth. Back to two cylinders again…then suddenly all six! What a lovely sound!

Stopped, got out, put on the panels and fan belt, and drove on into Plymouth without a problem! As we drove into the driveway, it was warm and sunny. Family and guests could hardly believe the tale of our experience.

The wedding was beautiful.

Two Turkeys

Certainly one of the true status symbols of the Depression which gripped America in 1934 was having a turkey for Thanksgiving dinner. I was 12 years old at the time; and while we had often eaten turkey at Grandpa Rohrbaugh's, we had never had a turkey of our own.

It had never occurred to us boys that the roast pheasant and rabbit we frequently enjoyed was probably better than turkey. It was the mystique of the thing.

By this time, Naperville had a movie theater, named the Naper Theatre, of course. Admission for children was ten cents.

You can almost guess what's coming. They had a turkey raffle night. Half of every ticket went into a barrel, and a drawing took place between the first and second shows.

I won a 12-pound hen turkey! It was a ten-block walk home. I was so excited that my feet never touched the ground!

My brother Bob had run ahead with the news—"Johnny won a turkey!" We unwrapped it, felt of it, and chattered excitedly.

I could hardly sleep that night.

Grandpa Rohrbaugh was, in my father's words, a "prince of a fellow." The following evening, he came laughing through our door carrying—a 12-pound tom turkey!

Well! We told him. He laughed uproariously. Chomped on his big chew of Mail Pouch tobacco and said, "Two turkeys. Doggone it. *Two* turkeys!"

> I was so excited that my feet never touched the ground.

❋

Grandpa Is Our Fixer

My Grandfather Rohrbaugh and his wife Cecelia (Celia for short) worked well together. Grandpa married Celia after my grandmother Emma died in 1920. My mother never fully accepted Celia. We called her "Aunt Celia."

Along about 1938, Grandpa retired from Illinois Bell. During that same time frame, we bought the house at 230 W. Spring Avenue in Naperville. This was an old house. No paint in many years, roof about shot, and windows in poor condition.

My dad walked up to the building, slapped it with the palm of his hand, and said, "Well, it will last longer than I will."

The house was quite typical for a frame house built about 1850 or 1860. The foundation was made of limestone rubble. The small cellar was reached by a narrow little stairwell off the kitchen or by an outer cellar door with a pair of sloping wooden doors covering the stone steps.

> **We soon learned why the street was named "Spring Avenue."**

We soon learned why the street was appropriately named "Spring Avenue." I believe there was a spring in every cellar of every home on the street!

Typically, I would come walking through the alley after school on a lovely, soft-aired October day and find Grandpa and Celia in almost a cloud of box elder bugs. If box elder beetles could find a place to crawl into a crack where it did not freeze, they could survive the year around. We had millions of them!

Grandpa and Celia had torn off the rotted deck boards of the east porch and were busily rebuilding the whole affair. They declared that they were, in fact, rebuilding the cover of an old hand-dug well.

They repainted storm windows and screens in season. They installed the wire clothes line along the wall to the garage. On laundry day, someone always took a wet rag and wiped the wire. Otherwise, there would be black stains on the clothes where the clothes pins gripped the wire.

He, with Celia's vigilant help, rebuilt the front porch rail, replaced the outside entry door, and on and on and on.

Celia and Grandpa cleaned out gutters, worked on the stove pipes, and at times, took their turn at rehanging the garage door. The "garage" had originally been a horse barn and tool shed. The swinging doors were just barely large enough to get a car inside.

My mother had a 1936 Plymouth two door sedan. The bumpers, which were an "extra," stuck out a few inches beyond the width of the car. "Ma" was an expert at catching the garage door with the bumper and flinging it into the yard or alley. Usually the damage was minor. When it was substantial, Grandpa came and rebuilt it.

So I, Johnny, summed it up for all of the family during one supper by saying, "Grandpa is our fixer!"   ✿

Forest Lawn

Late on one ordinary December day, my brother Bob telephoned as he often does. This time when I heard his voice, I asked, "What's wrong?"

His answer was slow in coming, and then he spoke something like this: "Arline died in September. We had been married for 30 years. Yesterday I got up my courage and decided to place flowers on her grave at Forest Lawn. When I drove through the entrance gates, I saw a large sign reading something like this:

```
┌─────────────────────────────────┐
│            NOTICE               │
│  All items left on graves are to be │
│    removed after ten days.      │
└─────────────────────────────────┘
```

"I didn't realize what it really meant until I was in the cemetery proper. People had placed wagons, bicycles, games, balls and bats, and on and on and on, upon the various graves."

We were both silent for a moment, and then I told Bob about the children's graves I had seen in Oklahoma.

It matters not if young or old. It matters not if rich or poor. It matters not if they have heard that story. Somehow they must accept God's promise, God's grace, God's everlasting, loving arms. They are not here. They have gone before. Rejoice and be glad!

Oh, if they would only believe. ✽

He Never Said, "No."

In 1934, the Southern Pacific Railroad despaired of keeping men "on the bum" off of their freight trains and coupled several empty boxcars on every train.

Men were riding the rails across the United States that year. Some were old; some were young. Some white. Some black. Some educated. Some illiterate. All of them had two things in common. They could not find a steady job, and they could not face failure any longer. The answer for countless numbers was to hop a freight, to go "on the bum."

Typically men would hop a freight early in the day and later jump off near a town where others knew of a camp or "hobo jungle" and sometimes a public soup kitchen. It was said that some engineers even slowed down a little at certain points so men could jump off.

Legend had it that certain houses were marked.

Many, many of these men showed up, with blanket roll or sack over the shoulder, at our back door on Brainard Street. Typically, we would hear a knock. My father would go to the door, and the bum would ask, "Mister, can you spare a sandwich?"

The answer was always the same. "Sit down on the step, old timer. I'll see what I can find." Sometimes it was a portion of our own supper. More often than not, it was a huge sandwich made with homemade bread and a big mug of coffee with Pet milk and lots of sugar.

Legend had it that certain houses were marked by the hoboes. Be that as it may, we surely had our share. But the answer to each was always the same, "Sit down there..." Some of the men were lousy, some unsavory, some half-sick, some crippled or hurt, and all of them very dirty. "...I'll see what I can find."

He never said, "No."

✸

Mabel Rohrbaugh Fry and Music

Music ranked high on my mother's list of priorities. She insisted that we all take piano lessons. Unfortunately, none of us "fell in love" with the piano.

I, John, played the trombone. Bob played the sax and oboe. Mark mastered the alto horn—predecessor to the French horn in local bands. Jim was an excellent sax man. Billy played cornet for a time. All five sons had a good love for music, and I had virtually absolute pitch.

With Ma banging that big piano and shouting instructions, we boys learned fast!

When my mother moved to Warrenville with her parents from the south side of Chicago before World War I, the upright Cable piano had come along. My mother was a good pianist—not a soloist, but she read well. She never went back for a mistake. She just slammed and banged through and kept going. With metronome tic-tocking and Mother "Ma" banging that big piano and shouting instructions, her sons learned fast!

All through our childhood, we performed in public often and well. Solos, both instrumental and vocal, were constant diets. The house rang with music.

Bob was our best performer. He started playing the soprano sax while in the third grade. At the age of ten or eleven, he was one of the best sax players in town. As a child, Bob was small. He matured late. As I recall, he grew at least five inches while in the Army. Naturally, he was often introduced as "Little" Bobby Fry. You can well imagine how he loved that!

Bob and I both played in the Amateur Hour contests in the park. Huge crowds of people stood or sat on the grass. The bandstand consisted of several wooden horses supporting a wooden deck. The lighting tower was an old farm windmill tower. Art Cline was the light man. Earl Matter brought his "public-address" truck.

When one remembers that we were in the heart of the Great Depression, the prize money was important. The first prize was $25; second prize was $15; and the third prize was $10. Bob always got first prize; my trombone and I came in third. By the way, we had the best accompanists in the area—Freda Druschel, Naomi Manshardt, Mildred Stauffer, or Miriam Attig. I don't suppose I shall ever forget the thrill of going up on the stage to receive my $10 prize. Wonderful days such as these made the grinding days of the Depression a little brighter. ✽

Memories, Memories

The years from 1923 to 1943 fairly flew by! Mother continued to teach school at Lisle, Illinois. Father continued as a painter and decorator. We five boys all sang and/or played musical instruments. We appeared often as soloists at church.

We brothers played at the ballpark, fought on the vacant lot next door, went to the beach, fished and hunted with Dad the year around, and basically got along well in school.

We were going through the depression years, and all was not perfect.

Brother Bill was a little behind in his class in school. In retrospect, he probably had been held back a year, especially as he was rather frail.

By 1943, four of the five Fry boys were in the U.S. Army. Bill later enlisted in the Navy, but he was discharged for medical reasons.

I, John, was in the 37th Army Field Hospital. Bob was in various Army units—the ASTP and other programs until completing his work as a medical doctor. He then spent three years in Japan in the Army Air Corp as a flight surgeon.

> I will pick up this cursory family narrative from time to time as I write about various life stories.

Mark was drafted at age 18 and served in Germany as a forward observer for a long tom battery. Jim served in armored divisions at Ft. Knox, Kentucky. For a time, he was fortunate enough to play in the marching band.

When the war ended, I returned to school. Bob also continued in school. Mark attended the University of Indiana Law School. Jim went back to school and then joined Mark in real estate, insurance, and land development in the Naperville area. ❁

The Fry Boys—John, Bob, Mark, Jim, and Bill (left to right)

My Father—Master of Many Trades

We lived at 624 N. Brainard Street from 1926 until 1938. The house was a Queen-Anne-style, newly built for us by Olivia and Scott Fry. It had a rather deficient floor plan. The large living room was along the south side with a brick fireplace on the south (outside) wall. The next room was the dining room and then a large, walk-in pantry entered by way of a rear hall adjoining the kitchen. Immediately behind the kitchen was a back basement stair down to the ground level and then from a landing to the basement.

On the north side, a large room was originally intended as a bedroom. However, when the family reached seven in number, it became our dining room, graced by a long oak table and light oak chairs. The table had been my Grandma Rohrbaugh's.

The single bath was located off a center hall which also served as an access to a front bedroom and a stair to the unfinished upstairs.

My mother used the downstairs bedroom. My youngest brother Billie slept in my mother's room. My father used the upstairs dormer room that was rather casually partitioned by Celotex-covered ceiling and walls. The other four boys slept in the large unfinished attic. Adequate windows gave good light and air. The floors were one-by-eight boards.

We had plenty of nice, big double beds from various Fry homes as Grandma and Grandpa died, and Grandfather Rohrbaugh married Celia Massey, a fine, hardworking woman a little younger than Grandpa. My mother did not really appreciate her. Celia was a big help to the Fry household during those terrible depression years. Grandpa fixed everything that broke around our house, did it all with an absolute minimum of expense.

When I was 12 years of age, my mother went back to teaching school. Mother was one of the few married women schoolteachers in the area. She got her job through the offices of Lewis V. Morgan, an old family friend who was the county superintendent of schools.

Bill, the baby, was just five months old. During the first few years of his life, Bill was in the hands of various people over the early years of his life. Merle and Edna Strohm lived near Wagner School where my mother taught. Each morning, Mother dropped off Billy at the Strohms and drove on to work. In the afternoon about 3:30, she picked him up and came home.

She drove a two-door 1929 Model A Ford that Grandpa Rohrbaugh helped buy. Though it had been hard used, it ran well and looked fine. With 21-inch tires and no accessories to maintain, it was a dandy commuter car. No matter what the weather, I don't believe my mother ever missed a day because of bad weather. She had four or six strap-on chains that could be installed without jacking up the car. They got her through.

I pause from time to time in my writings to talk about my father John George Frederick Fry. Remember, this is the man who was brilliant, handsome, laughed at adversity, and carried the nickname "Happy." Dad was an incredibly skilled marksman with any type of firearm. He could field dress a deer, elk or antelope in minutes. He could make a whistle with a pocketknife and willow twig in just a few moments.

Born and reared on a farm, my father spent most of his early life outdoors. He spent eight years punching cows in Montana. He broke horses, rode in rodeos, and trained truck horses. He could cook well in any kind of conditions. He also spent 18 months in the United States Army Cavalry as a mounted orderly to the commanding officer.

He and his father, brothers, and uncles were all skilled craftsmen. The family laid stone walls, built roads, built bridges, and on and on.

When my dad was sober, he was a wonderful person. When he had been drinking, all was different. It went something like this: He would come walking in unsteadily or staggering. In that condition, he just wanted to sleep. Unfortunately, my mother would yell and shriek at him until he was half crazy.

As the years passed, he drank more and more. It got so that when he had money, he bought booze. No one knew why. Only in recent years, in retrospect, have we who loved him come to understand.

My father was a painting and decorating contractor. He was very good at his job and was an extremely fast worker. Highly skilled, he taught the skills of the trade to employees and partners. They all became alcoholics. (The word in those days was *drunks*.) Society held that drunks became painters. The truth of the matter was that virtually all painters became drunks. The culprit was lead.

Virtually all paint had a lead base. Most paint was mixed by the user by stirring in and combining white lead, linseed oil, benzene, turpentine, and colors in oil. The pure lead came in 25-, 50-, or 100-pound pails. The procedure of mixing the paint was pure hard work.

It went something like this:

1. Gather all of the ingredients
2. Gather the needed tools such as a putty knife, paddles, rags, and some small jars or cans.
3. Okay, pry off the lid of the pail of lead.
4. Pour some oil into an empty pail.
5. Dig out the lead with your paddles and add it to the empty pail. Keep on adding oil and turpentine and stirring, stirring, stirring until you had the paint in the old empty pail and the new pail about the same consistency by stirring and pouring, stirring and pouring, and adding oil, turpentine and benzene until you had the paint ready to use or tint if coloring was desired.

The lead was about the consistency of cool butter. Great care was necessary not to add too much turpentine thinner. The paint had to be exactly right so that as you applied the paint with a brush, it would cover, adhere, not sag, not pull, and dry in a timely manner. People like my father spent a substantial amount of time every day just mixing paint.

Lead—it burned your eyes, irritated your skin, clogged your lungs and sinuses. When you urinated, it burned like the dickens and it smelled of lead and oil and looked white.

Now your system is full of lead and oil, and you have an insatiable desire for alcohol. Yes! No one really believed what was so obvious—lead makes drunks!   ✳

My First Restaurant Dinner

Dinner for 25 cents? Yes, dinner for 25 cents!

It was a Saturday in early fall. My mother, my brother Bob, and my youngest brother Billy were in Chicago's Garfield Park neighborhood visiting Dr. Bowman, whose offices were at Bethany Hospital.

My brother Billy was not well-coordinated and developed slowly. He entered school at the usual age of five years. His kindergarten teacher was patient, and Billy was well-behaved and cheerful. However, it was apparent that Billy was "slow." So we were in Chicago on this day to get advice (or sympathy) from Dr. Bowman, but no real help.

**Yes!
A dinner
for 25¢!**

As we left the doctor's office, my mother said that we were going to dinner before we caught the "L" to Forest Park and thence on home in the Model A Ford. (In 1933, the meals were breakfast, dinner, and supper. Some years later, they became breakfast, lunch, and dinner!)

We were excited! We had never before been in a restaurant.

The restaurant was only a short walk from the hospital. I suppose it was a typical neighborhood café of that time. Embossed tin ceiling; big, black-bladed Casablanca fan (probably didn't show the fly specks); marble-topped ice cream tables and spindly-legged chairs; black-and-white tile floor; glass candy and cigar case with a candy jar on top; large-leafed green plants in boxes along the window in front; transom over the door; fly strips hanging in the entry way; long lunch counter leading back to the kitchen; big, white, globe-type ceiling light fixtures; and, of course, a rack for hats and coats. It was wonderful, noisy, and exciting.

Now, the dinner. Just listen to what 25 cents bought! A slab of baked ham, mashed potatoes and gravy, creamed corn, applesauce, Italian bread served in a basket, oleo margarine, a glass of milk, a bread pudding for dessert! All this for 25 cents per person! All too soon we had devoured every last mouthful.

Oh! I almost forgot the proprietor. I think this was a one-man show. He was big; tall; probably fifty; with a big, black mustache; a big, white, fairly clean apron; and a white chef's hat. He was casually and completely respectful to my mother.

As I think back, I wonder if he even noticed us boys—round-eyed in wonder!

The price was right.

Dinner for 25 cents?

Yes! Dinner for 25 cents.   ❋

Shopping in Aurora—1934

Aurora, Illinois, lies on both sides of the Fox river about ten miles west of Naperville. In 1934, the city probably had a population of 60,000 people. It was a real center of commerce and industry. A partial list includes: Lyon Metal, Barber-Greene, Aurora Foundry, All Steel Equipment Company, Austin-Western, C B & Q Yards, Phillips Park, Aurora Golf Course, Penny Dreyer Clinic, Aurora Laundry, a world champion American Legion band, a YMCA, a YWCA, three banks, three hospitals, two high schools, Aurora College, and on and on and on!

We, as a family, went to Aurora about once a month (after my mother's payday) to shop for bulk foods, such as potatoes, sugar for canning, flour, apples, oranges, and anything we could buy in bulk at dramatic savings in cost compared to small packaged foods available in Naperville. Many thousands of folks did as my mother.

Downtown Aurora was truly a "Great White Way"! Picture this, if you will. The Fox River runs north and south through the center of the city. School districts and some political entities follow the east side/west side appellation as well, e.g., East High and West High.

Broadway runs north and south about a block east of the Fox River. Island Avenue, appropriately named, serves the establishments just west of the east channel of the river and below the dam.

We, as a shopping family, patronized a large number of stores along Broadway as well as on Island Avenue.

Come, walk with me down Broadway from New York Street and recall the street: beginning on the east side are these—Aurora Dry Goods, a modestly priced department store; next, the fire station; a saloon and restaurant at the corner. Across the corner, the Aurora National Bank; next, the Three Sisters Dress Shop, probably New York owned; then a huge fancy department store, Lietz and Grometer; right next door,

W. T. Grant and Company, a low-cost dry goods and clothing; next door south, S. S. Sencenbaugh, a real flagship department store—open staircase, crystal chandeliers, three floors and more; and the Merchants Bank at the corner.

Now, on the opposite corner, the flagship of Broadway—Sears, Roebuck and Company—a really big, complete-line store; as the Burlington tracks crossed overhead, they made space for small shops and stores.

Now let's cross the street: Bill's Hat Shop, Neumode Hosiery, S. S. Kresge & Co., Weingart and Pillatsch Haberdashery, a hat shop or two, and, on the corner, Walgreens Drugs, complete with large lunch counter.

Now a string of specialty food stores—the U. S. Meat Market, Aurora Fruits and Vegetables, a tavern, and downtown on the corner, The Tivoli Café with a five-piece band almost every night.

Somewhere along the Avenue were Thom McCann Shoes, Navarro's Jewelry, Aurora Poultry, May Electric, Northern Illinois Gas Co., Aurora Pants, Woolworth's Five and Ten, and many small shops and services, ranging from candy shops to beauty shops.

When my mother went back to teaching school, we had a 1929 Model A Ford two-door. Ma, as we called her, would load us in the Model A on Saturday morning, and we were off to Aurora. We parked right down town. My mother never walked; she trotted! She knew just what stores carried what we needed. At Grants, it was flannel shirts and denim pants. At Sears, it was underwear and socks.

Mabel Fry was a true shopper. Just before schooltime in the fall, all of the stores displayed new merchandise. It was new flannel shirt time! We started at the Aurora Dry Goods and then went to W. T. Grant, Sears, Woolworth, "Monkey" Wards, and finally, an hour later back to W. T. Grant where we each chose two shirts. That mother of ours had saved several dollars and got just what she wanted us to have. She was a real comparison shopper.

Now, we move to Island Avenue on the west side of the river. The west side of Island Avenue boasted the Aisle Theater, the Leland Hotel and its Sky Room, and the Aurora Hotel with its Hawaiian Room. On the east side of Island Avenue, Yetta Bodner's Blue Bell Dress Shop, Montgomery

Ward, and the Block and Kuehl Department Store pretty well used the entire block.

All within a two or three-block square area were City Hall, the Aurora jail, the United States Post Office, the YWCA, the Elks Club, the Old Second National Bank, Crosby's Sporting Goods, the Aurora Beacon News, the House of Vision, and the Tivoli Theater.

Last, but certainly not least, on Galena and Island at the bridge stood (and still stands today) the Paramount!

The Paramount no longer shows movies daily. The building has been restored physically, but the great, four-manual, brilliantly voiced organ is gone. Various performances and events are held there, but the nightly "before-television" days of a full-house cinema are, of course, long gone!

Downtown Aurora had every kind of shop, store, or establishment that might be needed or desired. One thing it lacked. *Parking!* Aurora's downtown depends in considerable measure on buses and trains. After World War II though, the ridership dwindled as "everyone" had an automobile. The National City Bus Lines, the Burlington Railroad and the Chicago, Aurora & Elgin Inter-Urban all lost riders, and, like other commercial "downtowns" across the land, downtown Aurora began to get shabby.

It appeared that the ownership of much of the downtown real estate was held by a few families who could not see what was happening. Why change or spend money? How could business as a landlord get any better?

Well, the axe fell when Sears announced that they were moving to Lake Street near Illinois Avenue. It was one big fat mistake! The neighboring stores were weak, and the location was, for that day and time, far out!

For the reasons mentioned and more, the old custom and habit of "shopping in Aurora" changed. Pace slowed. The lights were not quite so bright. Some said crime and petty thievery increased. Parking became increasingly difficult to find.

Finally, even for our family, Aurora no longer was a thrilling place to go. Beats me!   ✳

Radio

It was not new. It cost $8.00. It consisted of a box about 8" by 12" by 24". A speaker, hexagonal in shape, measuring about 16" in diameter, sat on the box. My father placed it on the fireplace mantle, hooked up the wire tied to the chimney top, and plugged the cord of the radio into the electric outlet.

It was not new. It was not pretty. But it played! Our home was transformed. Music, F. D. R. and his Fireside Chats, the WLS National Barn Dance with Bob Atcher, Red Blanchard, Lulabelle, Skyland Scottie, and Red Foley all filled the house with sound and experiences far beyond what we had dreamed. We had a radio!

I was about ten years old when the radio became part of our family life. For a time, only my parents were allowed to turn it on or even touch it. From time to time, Jim Kluckhohn, the repairman, came to our house and replaced a tube or two.

I suppose it is hard for young people to understand the overwhelming impact of the radio as I write on January 1, 1989.

I believe it can be accurately stated that commercial radio transformed the world with the impact of the invention of harnessing steam power, Edison's invention of the electric light, or the appearance of the affordable automobile. Suddenly, events of the day became words on the lips of folks across the land as Americans heard, "This is H. V. Kaltenborn bringing you the news of the world." Gabriel Heatter came on at suppertime with, "Yes, friends, there's good news tonight." Baseball games across the land came booming into every city, town, village, and crossroad.

For America at large, the greatest impact came with the hearing of the vibrantly confident voice of President Franklin Delano Roosevelt. Shortly after his election in 1932, President Roosevelt came to be referred to as simply "F. D. R." Early in his days in the White House, he began broadcasting his "Fireside Chats." The newspapers depicted Roosevelt at his huge desk before the fireplace in the oval office—glasses glinting, ever-present cigarette holder at a jaunty angle and his dog Fala at his feet. In the mind's eye of every person, that scene was set. The family gathered—almost huddled around the radio. Then came *the* voice saying, "My friends…"

Gradually, as the radio brought his words into the room, people's hearts were filled with a measure of confidence, a glimmer of hope, a thought that maybe…just maybe…the grinding depression that held the world in its inexorable grasp might lessen, and that there was yet hope! Yes, historians have come to realize that radio and the voice of F. D. R. came together in a marriage of facility and strength not often before seen.

> Radio captured the hearts of a whole nation of little boys and little girls.

Let me try to capsulize some of the programs and events that radio brought to us before the days of television. Listen! Hear that chattering clatter? That's a telegraph, actually a teletype machine. It is bringing a cursory narrative of a ball game in a distant city. The voice in the foreground is the local announcer "interpolating" the play with all the imagination and skill he can muster. Little boys like my brother Mark played their own game by the hour and announced it in great detail as they bounced an old tennis ball off a wall or up on the roof of the house. Of course, every boy knew how to get up on the roof of the house to retrieve his ball from the gutter.

Beginning in the twenties, radio became the new teller of the tales formerly and happily exploited by the dime novel and writers such as Zane Grey and the great tellers of tales of adventures of the late nineteenth and the early twentieth century. Radio made a hero of every "G-man" with gang busters. Radio captured the hearts of a whole nation of little boys with Jack Armstrong, Renfrew of the Mounties, Sergeant Preston of the Yukon Police, and others. There just can't be a girl child of the thirties who will ever forget Little Orphan Annie and her dog Sandy. The "Gee Whillikers" girl she surely was!   ✼

The Power of Knowledge

If a man empties his purse into his head,
no man can take it away from him.
An investment in knowledge
always pays the best interest.
–Benjamin Franklin

A Red Geranium

No, *not* red roses!

No, *not* one petunia!

Yes, a red geranium!

In 1931, at age nine, I was a student in the fourth grade at Ellsworth School, often called the East Side School because there were two grade schools in town—Naper School on the west side and Ellsworth School on the east side of town.

> I just thought that a red geranium would look nice on the window sill in our classroom.

It wasn't a holiday. There was no close teacher-student love affair. I just thought that a red geranium would look nice on the wide window sill in our classroom. So I bought one. It cost 35 cents. The teachers, Miss Betlach and Miss Lloyd, and others were very pleased.

I had already transferred the plant into a rather large, red clay flower pot. The teachers marveled at how fast that geranium grew. It was always just covered with blooms and clusters of buds. This was a BIG geranium—I would guess two and one-half feet in height and about two feet wide.

Soon the window sill held several glass jars of water each with a slip from the big plant. As the roots developed, they were transferred by the teacher to clay pots, and before too long, each classroom had a few geraniums—all descendants of that first 35 cent plant.

Many years later, after World War II, in the early 60's, in conversation with a teacher from Ellsworth School, I told him about the geranium.

He said, "You know, people wonder how long that old plant has been here."

I asked, "Are they still cutting slips off of it?"

"Oh, yes," he replied, "They cut several every winter and start new plants."

Guess what I am going to do? I am going to visit Ellsworth School and talk to some of the veteran teachers—what if?!

What if?

Stanley

Stanley was one of the first grade pupils at newly opened Ellsworth School in Naperville's central east side. We were a class of 27 students. Our teacher was Miss Davis. She could not make the kids mind very well.

Stanley was the tallest kid in the class. If you came anywhere near him, he pushed you, kicked you, tripped you, or knocked you down. We were all afraid of tall, skinny, white-haired Stanley.

Bob Steininger, always smiling, was one of the smallest boys in the class. We called him "Steinie." He was cheerful, well-behaved, and a happy boy except for one person—Stanley. Stanley kicked him, tripped him, and hit him and all the rest—a genuine bully.

On a chilly, damp fall day, as we were in line to go back to class, Stanley shoved Steinie. Something snapped! Steinie came out of that line like a wildcat. He came flying at Stanley—shrieking, yelling, fists swinging, tears flowing, and feet kicking. He was obviously in a rage the likes of which we seven year olds had never seen! Apparently neither had Stanley the bully. He got in a few hard socks, knocked down Steinie, turned, and ran away to duck into school to have his bloody nose fixed!

Kids had never before talked to Stanley. Now they laughed at him and made fun of him—no one was afraid of Stanley anymore! ✳

The Golden Book

I attended grades one through seven at Ellsworth School right in the heart of Naperville's old east side. The school was built in 1929. I remember the day that we, as first graders, moved from the old building next door.

School is school—sometimes frustrating, sometimes dull, sometimes hurtful, but mostly happy. One thing made it all worthwhile. You guessed it—*The Golden Book of Favorite Songs.*

We had assembly once a week when the entire student body gathered in the gym. No matter what the program was, we always sang songs. We each received a copy of the songbook. There was always a teacher or two who played the piano. Another teacher would direct us. We sang the songs in that book from cover to cover. Until I was in fifth grade, our main exposure to music had been church hymns.

> One thing made school worthwhile.

Then two things happened: I started to play the trombone, and we got a radio—our first radio. A new world! Take Christmas for example. I had always sung all of the traditional carols the year round. For me, Christmastime meant the sounds of Christmas.

I have always been able to play or sing in harmony. I was very good at harmonizing; I could make up a part while reading music with which I was unfamiliar. Let me pause to say that I could not play the piano. I took lessons from Mrs. Baer for two years from the age of six to eight, but I just would not practice. I do not know why. Still, my life was transformed!

Back to assembly and the songs in our Golden Book. I can probably recall all of those songs to this day. The names of wonderfully dedicated teachers come easily to my mind—Miss Morgan, Miss David, Miss Lloyd, Miss Betlach, Thayer Hill, Art Hill, Luke Short, Miss Jackson (my favorite), and, of course, Elmer Koerner, our band director. Almost all of the women sang and/or played the piano.

In retrospect, a happy coalescence of *The Golden Book of Favorite Songs*, a radio at home, and the coming of Art Hill as a music teacher and band director Elmer Koerner all changed my whole world to music, music, music!

But, you know something? *The Golden Book of Favorite Songs* was still my favorite!

Inattentive!

Report cards! I don't like report cards. I *hate* report cards. I believe that report cards breed misunderstanding.

As a student, I read voraciously. I listened intently if it mattered. I rarely took notes; I divined with accuracy what the teachers wanted. I looked out of the window a lot! But, I knew the answer before they finished the question.

Teachers reacted to my various level of attentiveness in any of several ways. First, they threw questions at me when I looked like I was daydreaming. But, I always knew the topic and the answer. Secondly, they would call on me to read aloud and then ask questions. That did not work either. Next to Margaret Worner, I was the fastest reading comprehension student that any of the teachers had ever seen. I know I infuriated my teachers to the point that they wrote *inattentive* on my report cards.

====
I hate report cards!
====

College was worse. Prof Finkbeiner, my German professor, would sneak up the aisle behind me and whack me on the wrist with his grammar book, shouting, "Fry, I knew your grandfather. He was a good man. Why can't you be like him?"

Each sentence was emphasized by a whack on the head with either Goethe or that old grammar book. His worst frustration came when he realized I was reading a few pages ahead of the class. In his mind, this meant "not paying attention." Then he had me. Next came a string of questions about the material which I had read ahead. I usually answered them all correctly. At this point came the real explosion—"Ach! Lieber Gott! He is inattentive!"

What can I say?

Many years later after a devastating heart attack and some other troubles, I don't often anticipate the question before the speaker can voice it. I do not necessarily view this as an improvement. As I think back to my "inattentive" days, I now realize that I didn't fully understand at the time.

It would have helped me to know something that faculty members and student counselors never revealed. For example, it was much later that I came to know that in 1940 as a freshman, I had the highest reading comprehension score ever graded at North Central College. Why keep that fact a secret!?

My whole reaction to many of the "inattentive" judgments would have been different if I had known in all of my school days that in some areas of study I excelled far beyond those "inattentive daydreamer" tags hung on my report cards. I have, to some extent, learned to live with this.

My wife Laura has berated me for years for interrupting others in conversation. It happens something like this: A person begins to speak. At some point between the first word and the question or statement, I know what the person is going to say. Therefore, I answer the question or reply to their statement.

I read in like manner. Many times the first word or words tell me what the page will say, and I "read" the whole paragraph or page in a long glance. Question me about the page, and soon see that I comprehend what is written and before me.

Well, as I said early on, "I hate report cards." I guess it is because I still have trouble not interrupting people in conversation! It helps just to tell someone about the times I had been labeled "inattentive."   ❁

Burlington

"Burlington what?"

"Burlington High School."

"Where is Burlington High School?"

"Somewhere out in Kane County, west of Elgin, Illinois."

"So what?"

The "so-what" is that I was recently invited to chair a special group of students at Burlington High School in a discussion of wars and "what about" wars. The time frame was roughly the Spanish-American War to Vietnam. Plenty of room just to talk about wars...wars...wars!

The seven kids were fully involved immediately. It was one of those special experiences when "time flies."

We flew all over the landscape as we traced the history of military rifles all the way to Winston Churchill's, "Don't ever, ever, ever, ever give in! If you are right, don't give in!"

I felt showered with questions about the story of field hospitals. As we sat on the floor talking about the crackly old pictures from another day and time, the questions fairly flew. I guess we talked about everything from life in the jungle to the miracle of American industry as 100,000 airplanes were built in 1944.

I think most of the group understood Admiral Yamamoto when, after Pearl Harbor in the flush of early success, he said, "I fear we have only awakened a sleeping giant and filled him with a terrible resolve."

"New Guinea," "North Africa," "D-Day," and on and on came into the conversation as the kids from Burlington questioned and listened.

I digressed but once to say in reassurance, "Over the years as you look back in memory, most of your troubles will be forgotten. The happy memories will remain in your heart."

You know, I felt that they were glad I was there!

Cleary

It was an old building. The owner-founder, Mr. Patrick Cleary, now in his 80's or 90's was still on the scene. Creaking maple floors, acres of oak trim, hissing steam radiators, winding stairs from floor to floor, big, old lights; a really fine and well-cared-for style of the late 1800's.

Quite a unique place—hundreds of typewriters, comptometers, adding machines, and educators were in evidence wherever you went. Guess what? This was a "how-to-do-it" school.

Their biggest problem was singular. Employers of every ilk came to the campus and hired the most experienced students away. The war was over. The big plants were converting back to peacetime manufacturing and service. Employers came seeking female office managers. They "stole" them by the score.

In that day and time, everything was typed. There were no recorders or copying machines. Mimeograph machines required a typed stencil on special paper and then cranked over an inked roll. Office machines were operated by crank or handle or keyboard buttons.

Cleary College is in Ypsilanti, Michigan, located about 40 or 45 miles southwest of Detroit. In 1946, Ypsilanti was a town of about 15,000 people. It was home to Ypsilanti Teachers' College as well as to Cleary College.

Cleary is a unique school. In 1946 when I first looked at Cleary, it seemed like a step back in time. It was an accredited four-year business college. They also offered two-year certificates in a number of different specialized curricula.

A friend of the family in nearby Plymouth, Michigan, taught accounting at Cleary. I really wasn't much interested. I was planning on attending the University of Michigan at nearby Ann Arbor. I went there as a freshman on registration day and found a line of prospective students numbering 24,000 and still counting. I left, and went to look at Cleary.

Listen to this…only a few hundred students…the girls outnumbered the men…a big, old, three-story building in downtown Ypsilanti!

We "took" a wild variety of courses. Some chuckled at the amazing course offerings: shorthand, typing, business law, accounting, office practices, speech, English, business letter writing, Roberts' Rules, and on and on. Everything at Cleary was designed to bolster one premise; namely, you can't really expect to teach or explain it unless you can do it yourself.

Another thing, if you maintained a "C" average or better, you could take as many as 24 quarter hours. I really sailed!

Mr. Kilian taught "Business Arithmetic." All was done in 10's and converted as in the modern math of years later. No dumb "carry-this, take that away, divide this," etc. Just add in 10's. Incredible!

If you misspelled any words on a paper—bang! You found yourself in a repeat special class—No credit!

Cost Accounting—total mystery. Should have been asked to repeat it. Someone in the hierarchy saw the name "Fry" and gave a "B" to me. To this day, Cost Accounting is still a mystery!

We had to take shorthand at 120 words per minute. Believe that? I did it! Type 60 words per minute? They said I did. I think again that perhaps the name "Fry" helped. Might as well face it—they liked me!

Some profs that I still remember are Lt. General Owen J. Cleary, Attorney Wein, Attorneys Johnson and Fink, Practicing CPA Don Sutherland from nearby Plymouth (Laurabelle's hometown), Chancellor Don Hutchinson who taught speech and wherever he was needed, Vice President Hadley—a good guy! Made things go from day to day. I can "see" many faces, but I cannot remember all of the names.

All in all, Cleary College, the "how-to-do-it" school sent me into the business world with a toolbox of tasks and the ability to use them.   ✱

Claude C. Pinney

He bought small wooden batons by the gross. In cold weather, he wore a great Oxford-grey cape. Impatient of any companion, he walked at a furious pace. Bald-headed. Not tall. Medium voice. Metal-rimmed glasses. Wore a vest; always, at work.

What did he require? Perfection! What did he get? Well...we came close.

The sounds that came out of Prof's students were, in those grim depression years, rays of heavenly sunshine.

He taught piano and organ, masterfully directed the Chapel Choir, and directed the mixed chorus.

Fall enrollment at North Central College (N.C.C.) was after Labor Day, and within days, choirs, choruses, etc. had become prime extracurricular activities. Then, by audition, the Chapel Choir of 24 voices was formed. Professor Pinney himself directed the Chapel Choir. I was admitted as a tenor.

Twenty-four voices. Well-balanced. Mostly upperclassmen. Accompanied by post-graduate student Bob Hieber on the great four-manual Kimball organ. So much music! Probably, this was the heyday of the musical enterprises at North Central.

Chapel Choir practiced weekly and sang thrice weekly. We were seated in the balcony of Pfeiffer Hall. Dedicated in 1929, Pfeiffer was a masterpiece building of great facility. Here Prof was at his best! An arrangement of mirrors made it possible for Hieber to catch Prof's directions.

In those days, compulsory chapel services were held on Monday, Wednesday, and Friday mornings. As I recall, most services began and/or ended with prayer. I believe the majority of the speakers or preachers spoke on Christian-related themes. Of course, there were the expected "all-school" announcements.

In retrospect, I doubt that the school administrators realized the impact and strength of the "available-to-all" conservatory setting and atmosphere. Prof was a key person in the whole effort to bring good music, impeccably performed, to the students and, in turn, to each student's sphere of influence—then and later. The sounds that came out of Prof's students were, in those grim depression years, rays of heavenly sunshine.

Prof was high-strung. Do it wrong or fail to get it right and one of those expendable batons would come "zinging" your way as Prof screeched and went into a sort of music-flying, chair-overturned, yelling tirade. He wanted perfection! To him, that meant singing like it was written. You couldn't just come close! You had to get it right—as written!

Prof coached the 1941 Men's Octette in preparation for the final summer tour. We were not outstanding musicians, but we got it all right! A repertoire of 32 numbers committed to memory challenged us all. I will never forget those 133 concerts with the octette. We blended brilliantly! We were good!

Prof never had an opportunity to train, coach, and send out another. Pearl Harbor took care of that. To this day, I don't know if Prof fully realized the impact he made on the memories of us all.

How could he possibly know what happened when shy Johnny Fry received his score of "The Messiah" and suddenly, after a rap of the baton, heard for the first remembered time, "For unto us a child is born..."?

How could he possibly know how a frail lovely, dark-haired, dark-eyed girl worked assiduously to perfect her organ technique to play "just like Prof"?

How could he possibly know that fifty-some years later a quartet out of the old 1941 octette would come together and, at a North Central gathering sing, "Homing" just as he taught us?

How could he possibly know? Maybe—   ✺

Class of 1940—
Fiftieth High School Reunion

I, John Fry, am one of the 99 graduates of Naperville High School class of 1940. For most of us, graduation meant a year or two of college or a job and then into the military service.

Actually, very few found employment. Jobs were still hard to find. After some minor yearly gains in the mid-thirties, the Depression settled over the land again. In 1938, the unemployment rate was about 80 percent. Truthfully, it does not matter if that figure is incorrect, "things" were awful.

> **The hours passed all too quickly, and soon it was time to part.**

So many young people went to college for lack of anything more rewarding to do. You could not plan a future. Then came the war, and the Naperville class of 1940, like classes everywhere, was scattered around the world.

In 1989, several former classmates met and planned a fiftieth anniversary reunion. The group included Ginnie Beidelman, Bob Feldott, Doris Knoch, Herb Matter, Katie Ory, Irene Osterland, Bob Sprague, Marge Staffeldt, and me. Others were present whom I cannot remember.

It all worked out. They say Bob Sprague was the driving force. "Good work, Bob!" For those of you who could not attend the reunion, it went something like this:

Friday evening—cocktails and a wonderful buffet dinner at Bob and Pat Millers. I cannot recall any details, but I know I have never seen a happier crowd. I think I was there?! Just happy!

Saturday morning—two Naperville school buses for the big crowd. I served as navigator guide in Bus #1, and Herbie was in charge of Bus #2. About 9:00 A.M., we started the local tour and stopped at the Church of the Brethren where the Naperville Men's Glee Club was rehearsing. I had warned Bonnie Klee, our director, that we might stop. We did!

The bus emptied as the classmates entered and found seats in the sanctuary where the rehearsal was about to begin. I introduced the two groups to each other. The Glee Club members were surprised; the reunion folks were even more surprised. I spoke about our commonality of background and spoke briefly of high school days, music, and memories. I also briefly touched on our losses in the war.

The Glee Club members took their places in concert formation. At this point, I said, "Listen now as I read a recitation called 'Men Singing.'" The Glee Club began to sing the haunting old Welsh hymn tune, "Suo-Gan," as the spoken word began to fade. And so it was.

We then sang the moving spiritual, "Steal Away." Next came "There Is Nothing Like a Dame," that exuberant song from "South Pacific." A song fun to sing and to hear!

Now they stood, Glee Club and classmates, as they heard the introduction to "The Star Spangled Banner." The members sang with the fervor of school days, high school days, college days, depression-year days, and the impressions of World War II. Most of all, they sang with the emotion-charged vigor and strength of a generation proud of their country and unashamedly moved by the patriotism which they proudly held. As the music ended, the two groups spontaneously intermingled as they thanked each other and then drifted back to the buses and back to the order of the day.

People were hungry! By now, it was almost noon. We headed to the John Fry family Tamarack Golf Club where the food from the Saturday buffet and supplemental viands appeared from the back of the buses. By the time all was spread on a veranda table and beverages were served, it was a great picnic!

Saturday night came quickly as all gathered at Cress Creek Country Club for dinner, a meeting, and dancing. Everyone seemed happy. Dave Little acted as Master of Ceremonies and did a fine job.

Sunday morning followed Saturday evening. I guess it always has! We met in a conference room in Fifth Avenue Station, which is the restored, remodeled, and rebuilt main building of the old Kroehler factory. I thought the appropriate song for some might be "Two Sleepy People," but no, everyone seemed to be wide awake for a continental breakfast.

The hours passed all too quickly, and too soon it was time to part. I have a fond hope. It is simply this: May it be that everyone had a wonderful time and all look forward to the new year.   ✽

The Triumph of Work

I look on that man as happy,
who, when there is a question of success
looks into his work for a reply.
–Ralph Waldo Emerson

Family Garden

We always had a garden. I mean a really BIG garden—rented vacant lots plus our 20' x 30' backyard garden at our home at 624 Brainard Street. Our house lot was narrow, because my mother had bought two lots and subdivided them into three lots. I can no longer remember the dimensions—if I ever knew them—but they were very narrow. The hen house and rabbit cages used up the remaining area.

The backyard garden furnished onions, potatoes, radishes, lettuce, cabbage, red tomatoes, yellow tomatoes, carrots, turnips, beets, rutabagas, pole beans, peas, string beans, yellow wax beans, individual squash, cucumbers, parsnips, a few hills of potatoes, and some years, a dozen stalks of celery. Oh, yes—kohlrabi, too!

In midwinter, the seed catalogs began to arrive. My father and mother spent hours studying and deciding on our mail order. We also bought seeds in bulk as well as in packages at Hildebrands' Grocery Store on Jefferson Avenue in downtown Naperville. We used vegetables from the garden from early spring until late fall and freeze-up. We covered many of the plants, such as the tomatoes, with my dad's painting drop cloths when the frost threatened.

Cabbage leaves, carrot tops, potato peelings and the like, as well as the weeds that were pulled, all went into the chicken yard or the rabbit cages.

We used a lot of potatoes. We usually bought them in Aurora in 100-pound bags. Almost everything else we ate came out of the gardens.

I had better branch here to tell about the BIG garden. We rented two 50' x 150' vacant lots about three blocks from home, just north of Ogden Avenue on the east side of Loomis Street. We hired a man to plow them with an old Fordson tractor. No disk. No harrow. Just turn over the soil. What I am saying is that each and every seed bed had to be hoed and raked by hand before planting. And, we fought quack grass!

We planted several varieties of corn, tomatoes, and beans. Pole beans were especially fruitful, heavy yielders.

Whenever we walked to the BIG garden, we carried hoes, rakes, and jugs of water. The only nearby neighbors were Abe Gushart and Jack somebody. They were old, bearded men who lived in a tar-paper shanty. Abe and Jack's only source of water was what they could collect from the shanty roof and store in a wooden barrel.

Most of the water we carried in our jugs went on the tomatoes and pickle cucumber plants until they became established.

> **Their only source of water was what they could collect from the shanty roof.**

Each time we visited the garden, we picked off the big, green tomato worms and stomped on them—barefoot, of course. Felt awful! We also caught speckled red potato bugs and put them in a two-quart mason jar. I can't remember why we saved them. I guess we must have drowned them because no one wanted to squish them!

When frost and wintertime were near, my dad buried the carrots, turnips, parsnips, and rutabagas in the garden under a pile of leaves with a few old boards laid on the pile to keep the wind from blowing away the leaves. We also cold-pack canned many, many quarts of tomatoes, beans, and pickles.

Really a lesson in self-sufficiency. We didn't waste a thing! Back to the BIG garden one last time to glean the sweet corn ears that were now dried or musty. We fed them to our chickens.

I wonder as I recount the tale of my childhood...how did we find time to do so many things?!

Different world!   ✳

Butchering

Along in the 1930's when the Great Depression was at its very worst, my father butchered a hog each winter. My brother Bob and I usually went out to a farm to help. Hogs weighed between 200 and 300 pounds live.

The butchering always took place in cold, cold weather. The cold was essential to the proper handling of the whole process. Upon arriving at the farm where Dad was buying the pig, the farmer and we would go to the hog lot to choose the hog to be bought and butchered. Once chosen, my dad and many times some other helpers would crowd it out of the lot with small, gate-sized, wooden panels.

We owned a Stevens Shur Shot, lever-action, single-shot .22-caliber rifle with which we were all familiar. Now, either Bob or I, depending on whose turn it was, would take careful aim and shoot the hog right between the eyes. Then, as soon as the hog dropped, my dad or a more highly skilled butcher, when present, would "stick" the hog in the throat. This was a difficult thing to do. The object was to slide the knife along the neck, past the shoulder, and into the artery. The tricky part was to miss the shoulder and avoid damaging the front shoulders. When done right, this process ensured proper bleeding. Some fellows were real experts at "sticking a pig"—hence the slang phrase, "he bled like a stuck pig."

Farmers always had some type of scales. Some used platform scales. Others had spring scales. Now the pig was weighed and paid for. At three cents a pound, the cost usually came to six or seven dollars.

Next came the hard part. Since my dad was a painting contractor, he had canvas drop cloths. We spread these on the back seat of the Ford car and then "rassled" the hog into the back seat and headed home. Once we arrived home, a neighbor or friend would help hang the hog on butchering gambrels and hoist it high enough in the garage to clear the rim of the scalding barrel.

We had a three-burner gas plate stove installed in the basement of our house. Its normal use was for heating water for laundry on wash day. After heating several copper wash boilers full of water, we carried them up the basement stairs a bucketful at a time to the scalding barrel. Now it was time to scald the hog to soften up the bristles for scraping. Scalding was accomplished by lowering the carcass into the boiling water with a rope block and tackle. (The same type of rig was used to tighten wire when building fences.)

Now it was time for the scraping to begin. Scrapers are concave steel disks about four and one-half inches in diameter with about an inch of concavity. They are bolted to wooden handles about one and one-eighth inch by five inches in size. The edge of the disk was ground or filed to a sharp edge so that when the scraper was pressed against the carcass and moved laterally, it cut the scalded bristle quite readily. As best as I can recall, a man could probably scrape a hog in half an hour.

Next, a round laundry tub with handles replaced the scalding barrel, and it was time to gut the hog. Using a large butcher knife, my dad cut open the hog from throat to bottom and began pulling out the intestines and all. As he came to the heart, kidneys, and liver, they were pulled and cut from the cavity and dropped into clean pails. The lungs were pulled out, things were trimmed a little, and after washing it all down, we finally had a clean hog.

By now, the winter afternoon was upon us. It was time to clean up, get rid of the offal (guts), and get the butchering table and tools ready for the next day. Sometimes Dad would split the hog right away. I think, however, that he usually waited until he was ready to start cutting the hog. In the meantime, he cut off the head and set it to one side.

Just look at the list of all the many products Dad processed from one hog:

First	—	Cut out and trimmed the shoulders and the hams
Second	—	Cut the pork chops
Third	—	Separated and cut the spare ribs
Fourth	—	Cut the bacon into large slabs
Fifth	—	Scrubbed and split the pig's feet
Sixth	—	Set aside the heart and tongue to cook as sandwich meat
Seventh	—	Soaked kidneys in salt water to eventually become part of liver sausage

Eighth — Piled sausage meat on the table to be cut into small pieces and ground as fresh pork sausage

Ninth — All fat and pieces of fat went into a big rendering kettle on the stove

When the pieces of fat were reduced to crisp pieces, the boiling fat was poured through a sieve into crocks to cool and become mellow white lard. Leafy fat around the kidneys was often rendered separately. It was whiter and appropriately enough called leaf lard.

All of the miscellaneous scraps joined the liver in the big kettle to be boiled as liver sausage. It too was cooked until thoroughly done and poured into crocks where all of the fat rose to the surface and then cooled into a protective layer of lard. Scoop off the lard. Dig out or slice the firm sausage. Ate it cold. Heat it as breakfast sausage with pancakes. Guaranteed to give you a "sour" stomach.

Sausage casings were scraped and washed, and the big black iron stuffer came into play. You pushed the sausage meat in at the top, and as you cranked, it ground the sausage and forced it into a spout and thence into the casings. Whew!

Finally the head! Head cheese! What else? Using a funny-looking knife, Dad would trim off the jowls from the head. These became bacon squares. The brains were used for brain soup. Everything else that could be trimmed off of the head was boiled into a gelatinous mix, and one more crock was filled with what was called "head cheese."

Soon after butchering, we either used smoke salt on the hams, shoulders, and bacon, or we took them to a farm friend who had a smoke house. Just think—live hog to finished meat products in a couple of days! Amazing!

Also, during the cold winter, we always had a side of beef in the outside basement cellar way. Cut off what you want and into the black skillet frying pan!

Singly, in pairs, or all at one time, father and five sons hunted rabbit, squirrel, and pheasants. We fished for carp, bullheads, chub, shiners, and crappie. We all were expert successful hunters and fishermen.

John George Frederick Fry was gone many years before we realized his veritable "he-could-do-anything" list of talents and experiences.

In retrospect, between hunting, fishing, butchering, and gardening, we ate like kings and never knew it.   ❀

Honey

Now! Honey!

My father had painted a large farmhouse north of town, and while working, he noticed honeybees coming and going from a large brick stove chimney. It was no longer in use. He talked to the farm owner about getting the honey. The owner said, "Sure, Johnny. There should be enough for all of us." Little did he know!

The next day at dusk, Dad tied an old painter's drop cloth over the chimney. That evening, Grandpa, Dad and I went to the upstairs bedroom. It had not been used in years. Grandpa Rohrbaugh knew almost everything. He watched the honey dripping out of the stovepipe opening. Grandpa turned to Dad and said, "Johnny, we may need more than these four washtubs!"

After a few minutes with the smoke can, Grandpa said, "All right, get the tubs ready." The two of them pulled out combs of old dark honey until two tubs were full. A little more smoke, and the "new" honey began to appear.

Soon we went for more tubs and, as I recall, we extracted almost five washtubs of honey.

We ate honey on pancakes, bread, toast, and just about any way imaginable all through that winter.

To this day, whenever I see or think of honey, I go back in memory to that night in the old farmhouse bedroom where once again Grandpa showed us how. Oh, yes! Grandpa left enough honey to carry the hive through the winter. ❋

The Kroehler Aristocrats

Really happy events or institutions come into being by way of far-seeing men and women at propitious times. Such Naperville accomplishments as the YMCA, the Nichols Library, Merner Field House, North Central College, the Municipal Band, Centennial Beach, Kroehler— the world's largest manufacturer of upholstered furniture—and on and on, came into being as thinking men and women acted and led the way.

The Great Depression was a terrible time in the lives of the American people and had a domino effect across the nations of the world. Times were hard. Money was scarce. Jobs were precious few. For about 40 percent of the available working population, a "steady job" was only in their dreams.

> **The time was right, and out of the ranks of enlightened men came the idea!**

Nothing seemed to go right. In turn, the country in various great areas suffered terrible floods, unbelievable droughts, farm family dislocations, "chinch" bugs, blighted crops, and silent mills and factories.

All of the resourcefulness and ingenuity of folks everywhere bowed to crushing failure as they tried to "make a buck."

Naperville, Illinois, fared better than most. Of course, the banks failed, and bankers behaved liked bankers! Of course, corn sold for 16 cents a bushel. Of course, hogs got down to three cents a pound. Of course, chicken thieves flourished. Of course, the dairy farmers went on strike and dumped the milk rather than shipping it to dairies who drove the price ever down. Of course, tens of thousands of men, unable to face their failure as fathers, went "on the bum." Of course, people began to believe that the big bosses did not care. Of course, thank God, some of them *did* care.

The time was right, and out of the ranks of enlightened men came the idea of organizing a really very, very good softball team. Eleven-inch, underhand, fast-pitch softball seemed one way to give folks some enjoyment and relief from anxiety and boredom. The name of the game was softball—eleven-inch softball. In the early 1930's, it swept the country. This was not a "punkin" ball. This was underhand, blazing-speed, highly controllable softball.

In the summer of 1933, the Kroehler Manufacturing Company decided to build a softball field and organize a team. They expected, and it pretty much came to pass, that most of the players would be drawn from the ranks of Kroehler employees. Rudy Massier, long-time Kroehler man, was put in charge of the whole project as construction superintendent, coach, recruiter, and general manager. Massier was a heavy-set fellow in his thirties or forties. He wore thick glasses. I believe he lived over near Naper School.

The instructions were to build a lighted, modern ballpark with bleachers, dugouts, fencing where needed, backstop, and basic parking area—no restrooms or facilities. The original, but basically unimproved field, was owned by the Knights of Columbus. They played regular baseball there. Several teams, including the Haas Brothers, played there.

The only lighted ballpark in town was aptly called just that—"the ballpark." It was located on a square block of land on the northeast corner of North Loomis Street and East Fifth Avenue. Today, it is a parking lot.

Parking for the factory trucks and lumberyard cars filled the southeast block of the intersection. Today, this area is used by the City of Naperville as a city maintenance facility with storage, repair, offices, and parking for city vehicles.

The site was well-drained, easily accessible and attractive. The east side of the ballpark was lined with big old pine trees; they are still there. The other three sides were graced by huge maple trees standing like sentinels on what are now the front lot lines or parkways for Loomis and Sleight Streets and Fifth and Sixth Avenues. It was really a wonderful setting and location. I am quite sure that the field was re-seeded, and in limited use that first season.

Rudy Massier hired a bunch of us kids to pick up trash, limbs, and stones. Someone trimmed the trees somewhat—it didn't take much, for silver maples are "self-pruning."

Building the ballpark went something like this: The 90-some-foot light poles were set by the City of Naperville Electric Department men using hand digging shovels 12 feet long! The city men used a gin pole arrangement and pikes to lift, guide, and pull into place the huge, two-foot diameter light poles.

The foreman or department superintendent made it all look easy. We, as barefoot kids, stood and marveled. The men chased us away again and again.

When a pole was raised almost vertical, with the butt end at the edge of the dug hole, walking it over the hole with the gin pole and guiding it with pike poles required wonderful skill. There was finally a moment when the pole could be freed to drop straight down. When the pole hit the bottom of the hole, the ground around shook! The City of Naperville Electric Department men were true professionals!

Now, men wearing climbing spurs and belts made many climbs to the top of the huge poles as cross-trees or cross-bars, wires, brackets, and finally lights were pulled up to the men with pulleys and rope. At last all six poles were equipped with the great enamelware reflectors, the wires from the pole to pole all meeting at a big breaker switch about ten feet above ground so that it was necessary to use a ladder to switch the lights on and off. The switch was basically a large knife-blade style. There were several great big fuses.

It took several evening sessions for the men climbing the poles to adjust all the lights to eliminate shadows and to lessen the tendency of the bulbs to "blind" the players. Those electricians did a remarkable job.

The above-ground dugouts were built of fir planks. Their roofs were covered with green, slate-covered rolled roofing, tarred down, and nailed with many galvanized shingle nails. The dirt floor of the dugouts was graveled.

The backstop was built of planks and spiked to posts to a height of about six feet, then continued on up to about twelve feet with chicken wire. The backstop, like everything else in sight, was painted Kroehler green. By this time, the ball park looked like a real ball park.

Ernest Overcash was a good carpenter. His sons Delmar and Harold (Red) Overcash worked in the office at Kroehlers. Delmar was a bundle of nervous energy. He and his wife Janet lived in a bungalow on Fourth Avenue. Janet worked at Kroehler also. They asked Rudy Massier and/or his boss if they could be granted the food concession at the ballpark. So it came to be.

Ernest, Delmar, Janet, and some kids like me pitched in at pitifully small wages and helped build the concession stand. While the stand was being built and equipped, Delmar sold stuff such as candy, popcorn, and pop from a couple of tables and the trunk of his car. Delmar knew how to buy the equipment, food, and supplies. He learned the concession and food business well as he made his weekly trips to Chinatown in Chicago.

Chinatown was basically an area of a couple of square miles centering on Twenty-Second Street and Wentworth Avenue on the south side of Chicago. Delmar delivered pigeons and squabs to various restaurants and accounts in Chicago. Pigeons? Squabs? That's right.

Back before World War II, when almost all farms had poultry and livestock as well as about 20,000,000 horses and mules, there was plenty of manure, which supported millions of pigeons, sparrows, and starlings.

My dad, who was born in 1890, said that at the close of the Columbian Exposition of 1893, the Chinese ringed-necked pheasants, common pigeons, British sparrows, and starlings were released from the great Ornithology Hall and its aviary at the fair. The pheasant proliferated. We also soon had millions of pigeons. A billion sparrows? Certainly millions of starlings. The pheasants became America's number one non-migratory game bird.

There was a bounty of one cent per head on sparrows almost everywhere. They were called "spotsies." As a boy, my dad had a Stevens Crack Shot .22 rifle. BB loads for the .22 cost one-half cent each. Each week, when his family went to the hardware store, my dad turned in "spotsie" heads and purchased more BB bullets. Spotsies were an on-going enterprise of his. In fact, he accumulated enough money to buy a Winchester lever-action Model 94 30-30 rifle. This was the rifle he took with him when he and his cousin Sam went to Montana as teenagers to punch cows.

Now—pigeons were good to eat. However, they built large dirty nests over clean hay mows and grain bins. They carried various diseases from farm to farm to which livestock were prey. In some fields, they followed farmers planting grain and ate much seed grain. Everyone hated sparrows, pigeons, and starlings who had all the bad habits of both pigeons and sparrows.

Back to Delmar Overcash. He was a part-time pigeon catcher. Night after night, he would go from farm to farm. Looking for squab, he climbed around in barns in the dark like a chimpanzee! A squab is a pigeon too young to fly but fat enough to be eaten. Once a week, Delmar went to Chicago with crates of squabs and came home with pockets full of cash. Pigeons were his real moneymakers. But, with the advent of the automobile and the power-driven farm machines, much of the manure food supply for these birds disappeared.

In later years, Delmar Overcash bought houses. I suppose he had 50 or so houses. It was his poor wife's duty to collect the rents!

So colorful Delmar began yet another enterprise as proprietor of the food concession at the ballpark. You can't run a ballpark without hot dogs. Everybody knows that. He sold hot dogs, hamburgers, popcorn, candy bars, ice cream bars, peanuts in the shell, and occasionally, taffy apples.

He hired me and my brothers, Bob and Mark, and one other kid whom I cannot remember—probably a Rechenmacher. We were paid a commission of ten percent of sales to "cover" the ballpark. This included the bleachers as well as cars parked along the foul lines and the outfield fence, which consisted of single planks running from post to post as seats—painted green, of course. Any ball that cleared that bench was a home run. Cars were parked just short of the "fence."

I can still remember vividly how tired I got as I trudged all the way around the park with a case of 24 bottles chanting, "Pop—five cents, pop—five cents, ice cold pop." Oh, by the way, after the game, we went out and picked up all of the empty bottles.

We always "ate" some of our earnings. My mother dressed us in clean white pants and white shirts. One night I earned one whole dollar! Delmar tried to pay me in coins. I refused. I got a one-dollar bill and ran all the way home to give it to my mother!

One whole dollar?

Back in the time when all of this occurred, the world was in the terrible, inexorable grip of the grinding Great Depression. A farm laborer was paid two or three dollars for a dawn-to-dusk day's work. Bread was ten cents a loaf, milk—twenty-five cents a gallon, a large soup bone cost five cents, and gasoline—ten cents a gallon.

School teachers were paid 90 dollars a month for a nine-month year. They, of course, were not paid for the summer months. *There just wasn't any cash!* One whole dollar indeed!

Earl Matter was an immediate descendant of one of the Naperville area's oldest families. His first love was flying. He built a primitive air strip on his farm southwest of town; charts from the 1930's and the 1940's show Matter Airport. Gently rolling grass runway. Wet spot at mid-point. Overhead wires at the south end. Many local flyers received their first pilot instruction at Matter Airport.

Harold E. White, founder and long-time editor of the *Naperville Sun* newspaper, flew from there and kept his Taylorcraft tied down there prior to the building of Naper Aero Airport.

Earl Matter's second love was his sound truck. He took a one-ton Ford truck and built a box body designed by himself to serve as mounting for a generator and several very large loud speakers.

The Kroehler Aristocrats hired him to cruise around town publicizing the ball games; he chatted and announced the schedule of games at the ballpark. During the ball games, he parked his sound truck near first base and "called" the games, play-by–play. No noise pollution laws in those days!

Earl and his sound truck were kept quite busy announcing and promoting many events throughout the years—events at Centennial Beach, carnivals, Dollar Day sales, Wheatland Plowing Match, North Central College Cardinals football games—parades of all kinds! You could hear that sound truck message halfway across town as Earl kept up his chatter, played music, and cruised around Naperville, a small town of fewer than 5,000 people. He met trains—I could go on and on.

But Earl's favorite sound truck job was advertising and calling the Kroehler Aristocrat games. However, he had one competitor—kinda-like!

Johnny Martin was a handsome, dark-haired man in his thirties during this period. He had a voice like a baritone bugle, and my, how he did use that voice! He exhorted, pleaded, and barked from his third-row bleacher seat midway between home plate and first base. With his white shirt, big black cigar, and that voice, he brought a whole additional dimension to the games.

Now, what about the team? Who are these guys in the shiny dark-green uniforms with all that gold trim and lettering?

We have talked about Manager Rudy Massier. Even as a boy, I was aware of the hours he spent at the ballpark. He had an office somewhere in the Kroehler factory. He also spent considerable time at the truck garage just across the street from whence came tools, repairs, and supply services. A good worker!

Let's just describe the original team roster, player by player, in no particular order.

Joe Haas was one of our catchers. He was the eldest of nine brothers, and a wonderful player. As catcher and the oldest player on the roster, he read the opposing batters well. His throw to second base had the speed and accuracy of a Gatling gun. He was not as fast as he had been, but as a batter he was strong. I still recall his rifle-shot hits just over the infield—really a batter to fear!

It was often said that Joe Haas should have been a major league baseball player. He had a fine family and seemed happy in his work. Perhaps he just wasn't attracted to the lifestyle of a big leaguer.

A handsome fellow named Knudson was our number one pitcher. I don't think he lived in Naperville; he may have been from DeKalb. Next to Joe Haas, he was probably the oldest member of the team. He had a very unconventional pitching delivery—a very good pitcher.

Howie Hepner from the west side of Naperville was the other pitcher. He did a good job and, from year to year, gained better and better control. Hepner had a blinding fast ball.

Bert "Bertie" Haas, the youngest of the nine Haas boys, played first base. He was the best batter on the team and hit many home runs. I suppose you could say that in my eyes, as a 14 year old, he was our hero. After a couple of years with the Aristocrats, he was signed by the Cincinnati Reds and played with them for several years.

Johnny Kilb was not very big, but he really knew how to play the infield and second base in particular. West sider. Kroehler employee. Even-tempered and steady. Hit a lot of line drives.

Rolland Barnickle was a good-looking, rather short and stocky guy who really was comfortable at short stop. Just a good, all-around player. I believe he grew up and lived in the neighboring town of Lisle.

"Bud" Massier, as best as I can recall, played short center field. He was a slender guy who could run like a deer.

Jake "Doc" Thoman played left field. He was an all-around good player and hitter. You could count on him!

I think "Vinnie" Clemens played center field. He couldn't hear very well, but that didn't affect his brilliant fielding. Another product of Naperville's good old west side.

"Raymie" Baumgartner was an outfielder who played right field. He was fast and could really jump.

"Butch" Bauer was the second catcher. I can't really remember him—after 62 years, it isn't easy to recall every name and face!

Ed Lipscomb also played first base as backup man for Bertie Haas. A superb infielder!

The roster I list here is that of the first year team. A number of other players come to mind as the team changed from season to season. Among them are Eddie Doyle, who played third base; Rex Berry; Otto Haidu; Al Drendel; Florrie Rohr; "Otsie" Schum and Grant Graver. Frank Rowe replaced Massier as manager about 1938; a man named Johnson became Kroehler Director of Athletics.

Well, we have a ballpark. We have the team. The light bill is paid. Now, let's play ball!

Hot summer night. Not much breeze. Couple a thousand people. Big lights blazing. Batting practice. Earl Matter's sound truck blasting, "Roll Out the Barrel." Teams back to their dugouts, then out on the field.

Umpire gives home plate a final sweep with his whisk broom, stands upright, tucks the broom into his right rear pants pocket, and bellows, "Play ball!"

The crowd shrieks. People blow car horns. With anticipation at fever pitch, the cheering crowds greet their heroes with a roar that could literally be heard halfway across town.

The moths around the lights are momentarily distracted, and the lead-off batter steps to the plate.

We concession kids are in action in our white outfits. The crowd complains about warm pop. Johnny Martin starts his steady booming exhortation. The first pitch is thrown and, for a while, the Great Depression is forgotten. Home worries leave for a time. All seems right with the world. The Aristocrats are playing ball!

No story about the Kroehler Aristocrats would be complete without mention of "games away."

As a 12-year-old, I sometimes got the job of bat boy for out-of-town games. We played the Roseland Merchants, Joliet Rivals, Bismark Brewers, Downers Grove, DeKalb, Kankakee, and some others. Over the ensuing years, the list grew as other teams such as Bendix Brake, Champagne Velvet, American Match Corporation, and Caterpillar extended invitations.

Travel by furniture van was the "way to go." Big, green straight furniture van trucks powered by a big straight-eight overhead valve engine. Throw in a pile of furniture pads and a washtub full of ice, and we were ready to go!

In the years from 1933 to World War II, the Aristocrats "carried the flag" for Kroehlers. There was considerable turnover in player personnel, including some who are not mentioned in this story.

December 7, 1941, came and the Aristocrats were no more. But boy, it was a lot of fun while it lasted.

They were truly the ARISTOCRATS!

Mowing Lawns

We—my parents, four brothers, and I—lived at 624 North Brainard Street in a new Queen Anne from the time I was four to fourteen years of age. In 1938, we moved to an old, two-story frame house at 230 West Spring Avenue, just west of the old high school. It wasn't much of a house, but the location was great.

While living on Brainard Street, I worked at a number of things to earn money. I sold pop, ice cream, and candy bars at nearby Kroehler Park, the home of the fast-speed softball team sponsored by the Kroehler Manufacturing Company and known as the Aristocrats.

For two years, I was bat boy for the Aristocrats for their away games. We traveled by furniture van truck equipped with benches and furniture-moving pads.

From age 12 to 14, I caddied at the Naperville Country Club. Didn't make much money at that! Fifty years later, our family enterprise built a golf course and clubhouse—I should have known better! Golfers expect a lot for their money—a lot!

Income from my chickens and rabbits amounted to several dollars per year.

I had a delivery route for the *Downtown Chicago Shopper*, a newspaper-sized give-away paper. It paid well. I used my bike for that job. All of my deliveries were on the west side of Naperville.

Magazine sales commissions were my only source of winter income. I went door to door with the magazines. Sales at the train station were always pretty good. My brother Bob and I went there at 5:00 A.M. and back again at 4:50 P.M. for a couple of hours.

As you can see, my brothers and I always had a little cash flow. Also, Bob never ran out of money. I never figured that out. It is still true 60 years later!

The whole point of this story is to talk about mowing lawns, and I'm finally getting around to that.

I had three regular lawn mowing jobs. Joe Lindblad, a wonderful man, owned two houses and lived at the northwest corner of North Brainard Street and Sixth Avenue. The home was a buff-colored, brick bungalow. The garage was on the alley. The Lindblads had little or no garden, so it was a large lawn, including the parkway on two sides. I cut it weekly at 50 cents per mowing. It took me about an hour and half. It took so long because of what we called "wiregrass." In this day and age, it is called "crabgrass."

Mr. Lindblad furnished the mower and had the blades sharpened every spring. It, of course, was a reel-type push mower. The only way to mow that wiregrass was to back up, spin the blades backward with your toe, and lunge, lunge, lunge repeatedly. A successful lunge went about four feet before the blades clogged again.

Not everyone had a refrigerator. The Lindblads did. One day, Mrs. Lindblad was sitting on the swing, watching me mow. (In retrospect, how bored can a person get? Kinda' like going over to the service station and watching the guy repair tires!) She couldn't help but notice how hot I was. I believe we always said, "Sweating like a mule." In any event, Mrs. Lindblad offered me a glass of ice water. It was so good! I never again mowed that lawn without going to the back door and asking for ice water. Guess what? Near the summer's end, she also gave me two cookies every week—this in the heart of the Great Depression.

The other Lindblad house was a brick, two-story home occupied by the Sankey Good family. I believe he was a postmaster. Joe Lindblad and his wife were related to the Goods. That lawn was small and had no wiregrass. I did, however, have to catch the grass. I do not remember what he paid me, but I do remember that Mr. Good died.

One day as I was mowing along the back walk leading to the garage on the alley, I met a very pretty girl wearing a velvet dress with a white collar, a round sort of a bowl-shaped hat, and white shoes. She looked like a princess. (As I am writing this chapter, I phoned that girl, Mrs. John [Anne] Lord, and told her I still remember her as the princess in the velvet dress.)

Down on South Columbia Street, just north of Chicago Avenue at the corner of Van Buren and Columbia, there lived two older widow ladies, Mrs. Breitwieser and Mrs. Seager, whose lawns I mowed.

I used to turn our family mower upside down, tie it to the back of my bike, and tow it clear down there. Sometimes I walked and pulled the mower by hand. Long trip!

Mrs. Seager's lawn was heavily shaded by many trees and was easy to mow. The heavy shade did not encourage a good "stand" of grass. She paid me 30 cents.

Mrs. Breitwieser had a somewhat larger lawn. Lots of shrubs, flowers, and trees. I can't remember what she paid, probably 50 cents. She was terribly lonely. Sometimes, she made lunch for me. It was always boiled beef, potatoes, beans, bread, and iced tea. She loaded up my plate and then sat and talked to me, eating very little herself.

So, I mowed those four lawns every week, or as needed, all summer. Doesn't seem like much money now, but back at that time, a man earned about $3.00 per day. On an hourly basis, my pay was okay.

When we moved across town to Spring Avenue, I no longer mowed lawns.

I still remember "Princess" Anne in her velvet dress, Mrs. Lindblad and her ice water and cookies, and Mrs. Breitwieser and her big noontime dinners for me.

Bless them all!   ✱

Pitching Bundles

From the mid-1800's until after World War II, most small grains such as wheat, barley, and oats were threshed with separators, commonly called threshing machines. Early on, they were powered by horsepower as teams of horses went round and round in circles, powering a geared wheel which in turn powered a tumbling rod that powered the big main threshing belt. That belt in turn powered the straw walkers, the fan, the elevators, and the straw blowers. Really, the old-time separators were a marvel of ingenuity.

The exciting years began with the advent of the steam traction engine. The availability of so much power engendered the design and production of very sophisticated machines. However, until the advent of the grain combine, getting the bundles of grain from the reaper to the separator was just plain hard labor.

The reaper machine cut the grain and laid it on a table. A powered canvas apron moved the grain laterally to a bundle rack or arm and thence to a tie and knotter. Finally, it kicked the bundle off the machine onto the grain stubble.

The bundles would have some green grass and weeds mixed with the straw and heads of grain. Next came the job of shocking the grain bundles. It was done as follows:

Grab a bundle in each hand with the heads up.

Set them butt first on the ground leaning in snugly against each other, six bundles in all.

Lay a seventh bundle lengthwise along the top of the six upright bundles, sort of like a roof to shed rainwater.

Some days or even weeks later, the "threshing ring" (a neighborhood group) arrived and set up. Getting set up and organized to thresh grain took no little expertise and was a lot of work. You needed:

One separator threshing machine

One big steam tractor (or in later years, a big gasoline-fueled tractor)

A water wagon

A coal wagon (some engines had a special firebox and burned straw)

Two grain wagons to a team

Four to eight hay racks and teams, depending on the size of the separator

An engineer

A fireman

Two men unloading bundles into the separator

Now, finally, men to load the bundles from the shocks onto the hay racks.

Most hay racks had a ladder-like upright rack front and rear. Some farmers had a man on the rack building the load.

Between the ages of 15 and 17, I pitched bundles onto racks of every size and description—some high, some low, and some "tippy."

Each bundle pitcher worked with the same team of horses every day. We guided the team by talking to them. "Get up." "Giddy up." "Whoa." "Gee." "Haw." "Whoa back." "Come on, Nell." "Annie, giddy up," etc, The team soon learned the routine.

The sequence of work went something like this:

Harness and water your team

Walk them to the wagons and hitch up

Get your forks, hat, and gloves

Head out to the rows of shocks and get lined up so you can pitch bundles from either side

Build the load with butts to the outside

Next load a layer of bundles over the whole wagon bed with all the heads facing the front.

Fill any holes and start cris-crossing the corner bundles so they would lock together and not slide off the racks. Load about ten feet high.

At all times try to build a load that is easy for the men at the separator to unload.

Okay, drive the team up near the machine where the men unloading could hitch up their team and take the load right in next to the machine.

Hitch up to another rack and back to the field.

All the bundles go into the machine head first. Try not to get too many green or extra-heavy bundles too close together. A good day or bad day depended on the bundle pitchers.

It was hard, dusty, "buggy," itchy, hot, sweaty, hard, hard work.

Threshing was a big event.

Huge dinners were served at noon.

After eating, everyone found a shady spot and napped.

All for $2.00 a day!

Pop—Five Cents!

The legend read "Kroehler Mfg. Co.—The World's Largest Maker of Upholstered Furniture." As a sign on the factory at Naperville, the legend was half a block long.

No one got wealthy working at "the shack," that is, Kroehler. There did exist a certain loyalty and pride in what they made. Different lines or price ranges were built. The flagship label was Valentine Seavers. When Kroehlers decided to sponsor a fast pitch softball team, that pride really came forth.

I have told the story of the Kroehler Aristocrats elsewhere. Now I am talking about pop—five cents.

Delmar Overcash worked in the office at Kroehlers as a price or cost accountant. He was eccentric, volatile, and tireless. He and his wife Janet had the food concession at the ballpark.

Menu

Pop	5¢	Popcorn	10¢
Nehi	10¢	Candy and gum	5¢
Ice Cream Bars	10¢	Coffee	5¢
Popsickles	10¢	Potato Chips	10¢
Hot Dogs	25¢	Hamburgers	25¢

Brothers, Bob and Mark, and I were vendors. We walked the bleachers all the way around the park where cars parked behind the outfield bench that marked the home run line.

On a slow night, we came to dread that long and not very productive walk. Delmar always pushed hard to sell "pop." It was made by some local man, and it was awful. The markup must have been great. I can still remember how discouraging it was to trudge around that field calling, "Pop—5 cents!"   ✳

Whispers of War

It is well that war is so terrible—
we shouldn't grow too fond of it.
–Robert E. Lee

51 Short Years

1990 minus 1939 = 51 short years.

Some saw it coming!

Some denied the obvious!

Some bleated and objected.

Most just hoped it would all go away—something like a bad dream.

America watched disdainfully as the Japanese Army marched across the ancient lands of China.

America watched and scoffed as the Anschluss came, built, and goose-stepped.

America watched the newsreel histrionics of Benito Mussolini, and short moments later forgot him as they watched "Popeye the Sailor."

World War II was at hand— why?

America accepted the God-awful convulsions of Spain in civil war much as they read Hemingway.

The early cries of Jewry brought shrugs, or worse yet, snickers and turned heads.

The sinking of the *U.S.S. Panay* brought brief headlines.

When the silly Mussolini picked on Abyssinia, King Haile Selassie received polite applause in Geneva.

The American Eagle stood and earnestly sought to inform. His patriotism was questioned.

The charismatic FDR trumpeted his hatred of war.

And so, the word pictures can be painted and framed.

Meanwhile, what of a tired, still-discouraged, depressed, down-home America?

They became radio listeners. They heard the maniacal scream "Deutschland Uber Alles!"

They became even more avid readers as they looked for a leader—someone to follow.

H. V. Kaltenborn trumpeted, Gabriel Heatter pontificated, news editors criticized.

The stage was being set.

The Maginot Line met the Siegfried Line "nose to nose."

Henry Ford sent a ship of peace. Annapolis talked ceaselessly of peace, peace, peace. General Lewis B. Hershey, director of the new active draft named euphemistically the National Selective Service Act, put into place guidelines for Conscientious Objectors (CO's), the framework for an alternative service program.

Everything was churning.

One fine day, the Nazi killers tore apart Poland in a new frenzy of demonic rage.

The world began to commit forces and got ready to kill 65 million human beings. World War II was at hand.

Why? Why?   ❈

Jim Wehrli

The tolling of the bells at Saint Peter and Paul Church gave awareness of the procession to the cemetery. For those awaiting the arrival of the family and friends, a certain tension began to build.

Singers, buglers, Marines—all stood at ease as the first cars and the hearse arrived. Now all assembled in their assigned formations and together with the Marine Corps Officer of the Day respectfully stood as the pallbearers placed the casket above the open grave and then stepped back to their assigned places.

A brother in Capuchin-style robe stepped forward and spoke quietly about Jim Wehrli as a family man and then offered a prayer of assurance. The priest spoke further in the framework of a simple eulogy.

Four bright-yellow aircraft flew over in traditional missing-man formation.

Prayers ended. The Naperville Men's Glee Club ensemble sang "The Marine's Hymn." The firing squad in full dress uniform fired three volleys as the sergeant commanded, "Aim, fire! Aim, fire! Aim, fire!"

The bugle call "Taps" now floated down the tree-sided lane with its tender, fading echo.

Now the faint fade and swell of propellers changed pitch to become a full-throated, snarling roar as four bright-yellow aircraft flew over in traditional missing-man formation at seemingly tree-top height and flew back—missing man high to the right—as they faded toward the horizon. My heart leapt! ❀

"I'll Close"

Bacolod, Negros Island…1945…Philippine Campaign…37th Field Hospital…Old Baptist Mission Buildings…Midnight—2400 hours…

Sergeant of the guard passes by the operating room or stops and gains a memory never to be erased…

Come back with me just for a few minutes to the screened door just outside that operating room. It is hot and humid. Insects cover the screen. It is very quiet. Medics sit in the wards at their packing crate desks. An occasional night bird speaks to the tropic stillness. A distant rumble tells of artillery supporting the 40th Division in the hills.

Captain Neufeld sits, a picture of exhaustion, hunched over a sheet-swathed figure. Surgical mask now hangs wetly around his neck. His eyes squint against the curl of smoke from a dangling cigarette. Pulled IV tubes drape over their bottles. With large needle and heavy suture, a picture of bleak dejection, he closes the belly-long incision.

A surgical tech drifts in, acknowledges the captain's nod, and settles down on a crate with pocketbook in hand. It is for him to watch and wait. It won't be long.

With a last desolate look at the dying soldier, the captain stands and goes out into the night. A short half-hour earlier, he had pulled off his mask, stripped off his gloves, and, looking at the sergeant, had said, "I'll close." ❀

Onward and Upward

During the second World War, another South Pacific beach was being won. On shore, one could hear from the supply ships in the bay the muffled rumble of mortars and see the black smoke of Long Tom hits on the hills above the beach.

A miscellany of barges, "ducks," LCVP's (Landing Craft Vehicle and Personnel) and LCM's (Landing Craft Medium) were plodding back and forth from the Libertys in the bay to beach areas to which they were directed by blinker signal lamps.

Alongside one of the rusty Liberty ships lay an LCM, one of many which had been there since the misty rose of tropical dawn. Four young soldiers had been down there in the sun, unloading cargo nets and piling cases, ammo, cartons, and vehicles. Now 13 or so hours later came the call from the deck high above to the four men in the boat: "Hey, we have to go in; we're getting whipped at the river. Come on up!"

"Come on up?" said one of the men. "The crane is working the other side of the ship now, and this barge is leaving. Climb that rope? It's 30 feet up there. The rope's wet! Now it's tight, now it's loose. We lie around on a filthy deck for two weeks, then work all day on K-rations—now we should try that rope? Well, here goes—around and upward—onward and upward."

The first soldier starts up. Pull hard hand over hand, pause a moment as line goes way slack, and then snaps taut as the two vessels roll on the choppy swell of incoming tide and crosswind. Okay, go again—hang on—grab the rail—made it! What joker said, "Onward and upward?" Boy!

Okay, Sarge, come on up, same story, leg curled around rope, hanging parallel as line tightens, clinging and holding as line goes straight down and slack—don't look down—slipped—get your legs around the line again—don't let go—hang on—where is everybody?—can't make it—"Bill, hey,

Bill, help me—Up! Too tired—"

"Heard ya, Sarge—gotcha!" Rest a minute—okay—let go one hand—now! Grab the rail—now let me pull you through!

Boy! Thought your number was up. Fall between that barge and the ship-side, and you'll be through.

Not much of a story; just another old soldier's yarn—some guy almost got killed—would have, too, if he hadn't called for help—that's right—called for help—where? Up!

No, not much of a story, but one as old as time, as old as God and man—"Onward and Upward."

One fellow was hanging on the rope of danger and loneliness out in the hills of Judea and he said, "...*I cried unto the LORD and he heard me; Unto Thee will I cry, O LORD; I will lift up mine eyes unto the hills, from whence cometh my help. My help cometh from the LORD, which made heaven and earth. He will not suffer thy foot to be moved: he that keepeth thee will not slumber. The LORD is thy keeper: The sun shall not smite thee by day, nor the moon by night. The LORD shall preserve thee from all evil: he shall preserve thy soul. The LORD shall preserve thy going out and thy coming in from this time forth, and even for evermore."* (Psalm 121)

Onward and upward. (Musingly) Onward and upward?

Another admonishes all—no matter the rope on which they hang—

"*Seek ye the LORD while he may be found, call ye upon him while he is near; Let the wicked forsake his way, and the unrighteous man his thoughts: and let him return unto the LORD, and he will have mercy upon him...and...abundantly pardon.*" (Isaiah 55:6, 7)

Soldier hanging on a wet line? Sure death below? Yells for help—somebody reaches down and hauls him over the rail. New story? No—old as the world—old as God and man—onward and upward?

Yes! Onward and upward!

You all either live and grow in faith in God; you all either live and grow in love for God; you all either live and grow onward—and upward—in love for your fellow God-created man—or else you fall off the rope of strength and help—down and away—apart from God—off the lifeline—separated—DEAD.

Sure, onward through life, upward on the rope of faith, the rope of strength—

How? How?

It's easy—you—you all—we—we all—have a Saviour. Everything is *all right* because when we *slip* and are about to fall—when we almost give up—we turn in prayer for help through the One Who said, *"Ye believe in God, believe also in me."* (John 14:1b) *"...When thou prayest,...pray to thy Father which is in secret; and thy Father which seeth in secret shall reward thee openly."* (Matthew 6:6) *"Seek ye first the kingdom of God..."* (Matthew 6:33a)

"Not every one that saith unto me, Lord, Lord, shall enter into the kingdom of heaven; but he that doeth the will of my Father which is in heaven." (Matthew 7:21) *"...but he that endureth to the end shall be saved."* (Matthew 11:22b)

We call for help and remember He said, *"Come unto me, all ye that labour and are heavy laden, and I will give you rest. Take my yoke upon you, and learn of me; for I am meek and lowly in heart; and ye shall find rest unto your souls. For my yoke is easy, and my burden is light."* (Matthew 11:28–30) *"For whosoever shall do the will of my Father which is in heaven, the same is my brother...."* (Matthew 12:50)

Remember when He asked, *"...But whom say ye that I am?"* (Matthew 16:15) Or when He said, *"For whosoever will save his life shall lose it: and whosoever will lose his life for my sake shall find it. For what is a man profited, if he shall gain the whole world, and lose his own soul?"* (Matthew 16:25, 26a)

He moves men to say—*"For to me to live is Christ."* (Philippians 1:21)

"My hope is built on nothing less than Jesus Christ."

"All the way my Saviour leads me."

"Eternal Father, strong to save."

"In the cross of Christ I glory."

Onward and upward? Onward and upward.

Alone? No, never alone, but with the help of God through our Saviour Jesus Christ!   ❧

Maffin Bay; Sarmi, New Guinea
45 Years Later

I wonder—Do the waves still pound on the long shelving beach?

I wonder—Do the palms in ordered rows still dip their sighing fronds in the wind?

I wonder—Is there still a faint truck track behind the beach?

I wonder—Do barges and amtracks still lie lodged rusting on the beach?

I wonder—Are the white macaw birds still as noisily flamboyant as ever?

1944; John (c) with buddies while stationed in New Guinea

I wonder—Is Wadke Island still a palm-covered splotch of white and green just off-shore?

I wonder—Can you still hear the drawn-out, jungle-muffled cry… "M-e-d-i-c"?

I wonder—"Will the memories ever still and fade?   ✳

Milne Bay

The scene—Milne Bay, a long, narrow bay on the southeast end of New Guinea. A place of palm trees, black sand, mosquitoes, smashed Jap landing barges and several thousand troops lucky enough to be assigned and shipped to the Southwest Pacific.

The time—February 1944, or more significantly, several months into MacArthur's leapfrog campaign back to the Philippines with the expectation of invading the home islands of Japan.

The weather—hot! Just plain hot! Wet! Just plain wet! We were there 33 days, and it never stopped raining. Water ran through our tents. Water ran over the roads. Water ran alongside the chow line. Speaking of that chow line—I nearly drowned in it.

A hundred or so of us were in line wearing ponchos and helmet liners with mess kits in hand. The bank beside me collapsed, and I was in the drink! I almost drowned! Fortunately, I grabbed a palm foot-bridge log, and some guys pulled me out. I did not lose my mess kit. First things first! Wouldn't that have been a hero's death?

> He typically led into taps prefaced by "Good night, Sweetheart" or something equally devastating.

Lifestyle—a learning experience. We learned to smoke clothes and boots dry. Showers were taken under a tent flap. The mechanics replaced sand-ground brakes linings on the 6 x 6 trucks every 4,000 miles. The never-ending scene of guys being shipped out in straitjackets began early on in our stay.

The bugler—somewhere, off in the palm grove behind us, a big outfit had a bugler with a big megaphone. We hated that bugler! It wasn't enough that he blew last call and taps. No! He typically led into taps prefaced by "Goodnight, Sweetheart" or something equally devastating.

We homesick sons really suffered! One night we heard from him no more.

What next? As unexpectedly as you can imagine, we loaded onto the deck of a Liberty ship captained by an 80-year-old Dutch gnome-like master and sailed from our tropical paradise to almost-on-the-equator Maffin Bay, Arrare, Sarmi, Wadke Island, and the *real* New Guinea.   �֍

December 20, 1945

Well, all things come to an end. On December 20, 1945, I was discharged from the United States Army at Camp Grant, Illinois. A nice kid typed up my discharge papers, and somewhere in the process I received a uniform.

I telephoned my mother in Naperville to tell her I was Michigan-bound to Laurabelle at her parents' home. Mother was not thrilled. Then I called Laurabelle and told her that I was on my way.

I traveled by train to Chicago Union Station, then by cab to Twelfth Street Station for a Michigan Central train to Ann Arbor, Michigan. Can't remember much about it, but it must have been an overnight trip.

When I arrived at Ann Arbor in the morning, I called Plymouth and, within an hour or so, Laurabelle and her dad came to pick me up.

Not too much excitement at that point—just too tired! ❊

John and Laurabelle, 1944

Sketches of Life and Times
After 1945 U.S. Army Discharge

I was discharged from the Unites States Army on December 20, 1945, at Camp Grant, Illinois. Sometime in the afternoon, I packed my duffle bag and caught a train to Union Station in Chicago. I caught a taxicab to Michigan Central (Twelfth Street Station) where I bought a ticket to Ann Arbor, Michigan.

Laurabelle was at her parents' home in Plymouth, just 16 miles away. Before I boarded the train, I phoned Laurabelle and told her I would be at Ann Arbor sometime the next day. I rode the train all night and arrived in Ann Arbor about midmorning on Saturday, December 21. I phoned Laurabelle, who had just put up her hair. About one-half hour later, we were in each other's arms on the icy train station platform.

I had returned to the real world some 20 days after leaving Mindanao in the Southern Philippines. It didn't really seem possible. We borrowed Alfred Wileden's 1940 Plymouth and drove to Illinois to see my parents in Naperville.

Mr. and Mrs. Alfred Wileden,
Laurabelle's parents

My folks and my two brothers, Jim and Bill, were there. My brothers, Bob and Mark, were still in the service. Laurabelle and I returned to Plymouth in a few days—Laurabelle to her teaching job and I to just sort of get used to things in civilian life.

About this time, I began running a low-grade fever and suffering pain in my hip. I consulted an internal medicine specialist in Detroit. No answers! In retrospect, I came to realize I suffered from untreated gout. Not very romantic , but not much fun either.

Soon, I took a job as a laborer at the nearby railroad roundhouse. We were storing sheet steel owned by the G. M. Corporation. They were in the throes of a 35-day strike and could not gain access to their own facilities. (Incidentally, the entire G. M. area enjoyed a startling jump in new babies arriving nine months or more later!)

At all times, I had planned on enrolling at the University of Michigan at Ann Arbor. The university had a 1945 enrollment of 13,000 students. On the first day of pre-registration in February, I found myself in line as part of a projected class of 34,000 or more students. I was overwhelmed when I learned that they were planning to flunk about 12,000 students. I was in a quandary.

We had purchased a hard-used 1940 Buick super four-door, and one day, while having some body work performed on it, I met a fellow who was attending Cleary College in nearby Ypsilanti. In later conversation with Laurabelle and her folks about Cleary, I learned that a fellow church member, who was a C.P.A., taught as an instructor. Off to explore this little old college.

A Mr. Hadley greeted me kindly. Mr. Donald Hutchinson en-couraged me and further indicated that they would waive some of the courses normally required for graduation. They were anxious for students majoring in business administration and business law. In retrospect, I probably could have gone on to law school. I never thought of it. I was too anxious to get back into the real world—to get started in a job.

Florence Bauer was a sorority sister of Laurabelle's at Eastern Michigan University. Her husband Jack was a reporter for Dun and Bradstreet. He knew P. C. McGinnis at Dun and Bradstreet in Chicago. I telephoned him, and he told me to come to work at 600 Adams Street in Chicago. The outcome of it all was that I was back in Naperville and working in an extremely interesting job.

I worked for 11 months on the near south side of Chicago as an investigative reporter. Next, I became a revision reporter in Kane County. I worked from home and had a very modest expense account. Finally, while still working out of the home, I was asked to be a regular reporter of four counties. Wonderful job, but it did not pay well. Ed Sullivan, my boss, said that the only way he would pay me more money would be if I would return to the Chicago office and be in charge of 13 ladies who did filing and specific manifolding of reports.

The I went to work for an insurance company. They promised that as soon as I had a broker's license and demonstrated an ability to sell, I would be made a regular ordinary agent. I met all of their requests and immediately began annual record sales beyond anyone in the district had ever done. One day, two auditors walked in, implied that I was not handling my books properly, and treated me abusively. I went to the main office to see my boss and quit! I felt no particular pressure about getting a different job because I had over $3,000 due me in commissions. I never got it. In 1954, that was a lot of money.

Meanwhile, life moved on in Naperville. Laurabelle and I, along with my brother Jim's help, built our first home on 817 N. Eagle Street. It was a modest red-brick story and a half house. It is still sharp.

John Alan, our firstborn, arrived on May 31, 1947 in Michigan. Larry was born on March 4, 1950. Gordon, our youngest, was born March 11, 1956. I have written much about events and activities over those years.

I decided to join my brothers, Jim and Mark, as an insurance broker and real estate salesman. I chose not to be a partner but worked as a cooperating broker. It worked out fairly well. After Jim moved to California, I was more independent as far as the real estate brokerage actions were concerned. Family business arrangements are not all good.

Soon after becoming involved in real estate, it seemed obvious that there was a market for lot and home sites. With this premise in mind, a friend, Glenn Vermaat, and I contracted to buy 30 acres on Hobson Road and quickly divided it into small parcels and lots.

We were wonderfully successful and very fortunate. The market was there, and we filled that need. Laurabelle and I next bought 50 acres of the Hageman farm southwest of town.

In the meantime, Fry Brothers Realtors moved from 212 S. Washington Street to 1020 Ogden Avenue, a building owned by Jim, Mark, and Al Beidelman. Moving to the highway location was several years premature. Traffic just zipped by at 60 miles per hour. We later moved to a new, but small, building at 25 South Washington. No parking. Too small. I should have left at that time.

Jim moved to California in 1957. Mark died on March 21, 1983. In 1990 we moved the office to the Tamarack Golf Club clubhouse.   ❁

Rest and Relaxation

*A vacation is over when you begin
to yearn for your work.*
–Morris Fishbein

Harvest Festival

My Grandfather Rohrbaugh was a long-term employee of Bell Telephone Company and had friends in "high places." I have always contended that the "good-old-boy" fraternity helped him get the job of superintendent of the Warrenville telephone company resort and rest camp from 1909 until his retirement in 1938.

One of the nicest benefits Grandpa received as superintendent of the camp was the arrangement for housing. He, my grandma, and my mother lived in a new three-bedroom, six-room house with a porch and a full basement. Across the drive was an oversized, two-car garage. Since the house was at the main entrance to the grounds, it was appropriately enough called the "Gate House."

Every year, the Church of the Brethren held a harvest festival. Grandpa's garage and lawns were the ideal location. The festival was probably held in September. Grandpa had lights strung. The communion tables from church were set up. Folding chairs were furnished by one of the undertakers.

The grand night was at hand. The church membership of about 300 was probably one-third farmers. Also, most folks had gardens. So, there were tons of melons, apples, beans, squash, pumpkins, carrots, beets, cabbage, and all the myriad of fruits and vegetables imaginable were on display all over the area.

By late Saturday afternoon, the dinner was cooking and produce was in place. Citronella candles were burning.

Now came the final touch—the baked goods. You cannot imagine the huge array of pies, cakes, canned fruit and vegetables, desserts of all kinds, and, of course, ice cream frozen and ready to be cranked. Indescribable!

What have I forgotten? Oh, yes, fancy sewing work, quilts, rag rugs, watermelons, cider, smoked sausage, dill branches, pickles galore, and again, on and on! It is amazing what a crowd of 300 or so folks can eat!

From time to time during the whole affair, there was always entertainment. We had talented people. Edith Fry, a soprano. She should have been a professional. She won third place in the Naperville Central Amateur Hour.

Connie Shaefer, singer, career school teacher.

Wayne Flory, piano. He is still playing with a big band in Atlanta, Georgia.

Bob Fry, sax man. Incredible talent. He won first place in the Warrenville Centennial Amateur Hour. He also won first place in the Naperville Centennial Amateur Hours. If it had a reed on it, Bob could play it.

> We took all of that talent for granted back in the days before television.

Johnny Fry, trombone man and tenor vocalist. He won second place in Warrenville and Naperville Centennial Amateur Hours. He was a guest on WMRO radio station, had the male lead in high school musicals, and was the youngest member of the Naperville YMCA chorus.

Elsie Barkdoll, chorister. A wonderful little lady with a powerful soprano voice.

Russ Witte, guest accordionist.

June Shaefer, dramatic reader.

Merlin Auner, incredible talent and voice—lost over Ploesti. What a waste!

We took all of that talent for granted back in the days before the television.

Along about early dusk, the dinner line had become a lunch line for the latecomers, the garbage and trash so far was in a farmer's flare box or grain wagon. The little moths are thick around Grandpa's strung lights. There is no more music. Little kids are playing hide and seek. Older kids are hiding together here and there, but they don't want to be found. Younger brothers can be a real pain! Just about the time the teenage couples found a quiet spot or the backseat in Dad's car, they would be found out by door-banging, yelling, teasing kids. Whatever the couples had in mind had to wait for a more propitious time.

Now! The eating and entertainment are over. It's time to sell the cornucopia of produce, the galaxy of flowers, the handwork and sewing, the baked goods, and the quilts.

Les Steck, a big, portly, soft-spoken, voice-to-be-heard community leader, farmer, and retail dairyman, mounted the platform and began his spiel. "All right folks, it's time for the sale. First, we'll sell the flowers, then the fruits and vegetables. After that, we'll work our way around, and last of all, we'll have the bake sale. Now we all know where the money goes, so let's get in there and bid. Johnny Erb and Harold Olsen will help catch bids."

"All right, let's start with that basket of gladiolas. Take $3.00 for it—take $3.00 for it. Take one to start it. Take one to start it. Dollar I got. I want two dollars. I want two. Dollar I got, gimme two. Dollar I got, gimme two. Two dollars! I got two dollars, gimme three. Three? Three? All done? All done? Sold the flowers for two dollars to Lou Schreiber. Next?"

The little kids are whining; there seem to be a few less teenagers. The citronella candles are guttering in their last puddle of wax. Les Steck is hoarse.

Some of the pies brought $10 as old rivals ran up the bid and showed off a little.

One lady says, "I don't think I want a Harvest Festival next year. It's too much work!"

Dora Shiffler answers, "Oh, don't worry. When next year comes, you will be helping again."

We'll make it the best Harvest Festival ever!

Hawaii

We, Laura and I, have visited Hawaii many times. We like it all.

We like the wonderful old Royal Hawaiian Hotel on Waikiki. In fact, the Surf Room there seems like a home away from home.

We also like the Kahala Hilton at the end of Waikiki Beach.

The Garden Café in Liberty House at the Ala Moana Center. Liberty House is one of our favorites. A real department store. They just seem to have everything!

Up the road a ways, we always go out to visit the Arizona Memorial. Helps to keep fresh the event of "Remember Pearl Harbor" era.

The lovely Aloha Tower seems a little tired now, but she is still home to the cruise fleet.

Stand among the palms and ponds—the scene as the Royal Hawaiian Band plays "Aloha." Walk south and find a seat on the grass as the Royal Hawaiian Band begins their Thursday concert. They are still a great old band. They are the Mayor's band.

Aloha now until we meet again.

Three lady vocalists are ample in size. They have ukeleles and sing the old songs and soon have the people in the "palms of their hands." Unashamedly sentimental as they sing the old songs—"Blue Hawaii," "Sweet Leilani," "Hawaiian Wedding Song," "Tiny Bubbles," "I Remember You," and on and on. They know them all! Comes the end of another concert and the audience stands. Holding hands with friends and strangers, the tears begin to flow as the band and the beautiful ladies sing "Aloha oe, Aloha"—a fond embrace. "Aloha now until we meet again."

What beautiful people! People in Hawaii smile and laugh a lot. Hard-driving "mainlanders" are often critical of what they view as indolence, a lack of drive, or yes, even irresponsibility. I disagree. There is something about the island people that is infinitely charming.

Have you ever heard a Hawaiian church congregation sing? How about "Holy, Holy, Holy," sung as a lovely soft waltz? Listen to "Great is Thy Faithfulness" as a sentimental ballad. How about "Silent Night, Holy Night" to the winsome chords of a guitar and ukelele? Try it, you'll like it! As you have seen by now, Hawaii is music, music, music! Frankly, I do not enjoy Hawaiian rock—too much noise and not enough music.

Oahu is home is Honolulu, Pearl Harbor, Waikiki, and a whole galaxy of enterprises. I hope your curiosity is piqued enough to talk you into a trip to the islands. With that in mind, let me tell you about a bunch of little experiences.

Years back, air traffic into Hawaii was handled by an old military strip and then a long bus ride around the island to Kona. We liked Kona when it had a jail; an old, old hotel; a huge mangrove tree; and one modern hotel. We like it just as much as a bustling shopping area with hotels and golf courses, and a big airport. I think it might be because of the carefree lifestyle of the Hawaiian people. One of our lovely memories of Kona was the Connie Francis Show. Still charming in spots is Lahaina. Typical hotel. Another old whaling ship harbor. Just fun.

The "QE II" is the old-time Cunard liner that has been in service for about 46 years. Originally built in England on the Clyde, she is the last of the huge liners. In recent years, she was refurbished and refitted and given new engines in Hamburg, Germany, as I recall. She looks like a real ship. It is sometimes said that when she is at her full speed of 30-some knots, she slices through the flying ocean foam like a great greyhound. Occasionally when going on in a world cruise or when being seasonally repositioned, she cruised the Hawaiian Islands. What great fun!

The North Atlantic had a mind of her own when we boarded near San Diego, headed to Maui, Hawaii, Oahu, and Pearl Harbor. The old girl was casually anchored off shore at Kona and Lahaina, and then went on to Honolulu and the Aloha Tower. Rides in a tender from shore to ship were wild. Frankly, I was really scared! Some passengers were injured stepping or leaping from the tender deck onto the service barge at water-line level.

Maui, the Kaanapali Beach Resort Hotel is sort of like a visit to Heaven! The grand old Mauna Kea Hotel dominated the big island for years. Robert Trent Jones Golf Courses and a world-class staff are there to please, and so they do!

The rolling vistas of the paternal Parker Ranch introduce one to a different world of obvious husbandry of the land. Cattle, cattle, everywhere!

At the risk of sounding like a travelogue narrator, I have shared some of my memories and Laurabelle's memories as we talk about a sampling of the islands. If you haven't visited the islands, for heaven's sake, do so.

You may have to wait for the "old man." You might not get an overwhelming welcome just anywhere. Sometimes you will have to wait for seating at breakfast at the Surf Room. Don't worry! Just relax and watch people!

Aloha!   ❋

Lordsburg, New Mexico

"The wheel is falling off," yelled my son Gordon. Sure enough, the wheel *had* fallen off!

"Hang on," I shouted, and everyone tried.

I steered the motor home to the shoulder of the road and held it straight. It was not easy! We finally stopped. Getting out was not easy either because the shoulder of the road dropped off sharply. We were sitting at about a 25 percent tilt!

We had come through the mountains safely just minutes before the axle broke.

We had arrived at Lordsburg, New Mexico. Laurabelle and I, Nancy and Alan (our newlyweds), and our younger sons, Larry and Gordon, were on our way to Arcadia, California, for Christmas. We planned to arrive about December 20.

In all fairness, let me take you back to how it all started. How did the trouble begin?

The new motor home seemed to be basically well-designed. However, it had an electrical problem. The batteries boiled and filled the unit with fumes.

We called the factory where the unit was built and learned that they knew of the problem and thought they had corrected it. They advised us what cables to switch. I tried to switch them and promptly burned a bunch of wires.

The owner of the factory sent his head mechanic in their Twin Comanche airplane. The mechanic came to the home of Elaine Davidson, Nancy's mother, in Wichita, Kansas, where we were staying. This was our first planned stop on the trip to California. That very "capable" mechanic worked for almost two days but could not get everything just right.

The factory owner then had an employee drive his own personal motor home to Wichita where we loaded everything into the replacement. And once again, we headed for California by way of the southern route to avoid a snowstorm.

The replacement unit seemed to be all right, although the engine should have been a little larger. More powerful.

So, here we were at dusk winding down through the foothills into Lordsburg on the twenty-second of December. It looked like we might be at brother Bob's for Christmas. But, as you know, that was now unlikely.

As Gordon yelled....

Well, we scrambled out of the motor home with difficulty because the doors on the right side overhung the ditch. It was a grade bank of about 30 feet. So we all exited by way of the driver's seat. The right front bumper was buried in the gravel shoulder, and the wheel was jammed up against the frame and suspension. The vehicle looked ridiculous.

When the tow truck arrived and picked up the front end, as the wheel appeared and could be pulled away from the frame, our problem became clear. The front wheel had not come off. The axle was broken! That was why I had not heard nor felt any warning vibration or noise.

When we got to the repair shop from whence the tow truck had come, the breakage became understandable. The manufacturer wanted a wide front wheel so he just turned the wheel inside out! You don't ever do that!

All spindle-type axles have a large inner bearing and a smaller outer bearing. The inner bearing is directly in line with the center of the wheel and is load bearing. The smaller outer bearing acts as pilot and end-play adjustment. The dish or depth of the wheel from the wheel hub places the load straight down on the inner bearing. As it was, all of the load was placed on the smaller outer bearing. It was terribly overloaded.

The little outer bearing got hot, bending and heated, so hot that it melted the nut, washer, bearing, and brake assembly. As a result, the vehicle literally dropped on the road.

We had been driving on winding, hilly, and mountainous roads all day. As the road became straight, we slowed down and entered Lordsburg.

We checked into a motel right across the street. Phone calls to the manufacturer brought instructions to have the vehicle repaired. I had learned there were no parts available locally, and we did not want to be stuck in Lordsburg. I told the owner where we were leaving the motor home and advised him that we would not ride one more foot in this outfit.

There was one automobile dealer in town. He had four used cars for sale—a Chevy wagon, two older four-door sedans, and a 1965 Mercury

Comet station wagon. This had a three-speed, manual transmission, a V-8 engine, and best of all, a full-length top carrier. Colorfully painted on the sides was the legend, "Lordsburg General Mercantile." The car needed rear window and tailgate repair, two new tires, complete servicing, and heavy duty coil spring rear shock absorbers.

We agreed on a price that was a little high, but the dealer said the car would be ready about midmorning the following day.

All worked as planned. We bought some kind of tarp, some tie-down straps, and yellow plastic garbage bags. Why yellow plastic garbage bags? Since everything was packed in drawers we had no suitcases. So we tied the loaded (and I do mean loaded) garbage bags to the top carrier of the little station wagon. What a sight!

We rolled out of town about noon in our grossly overloaded little car. It drove well and never complained. In fact, we cruised along at 65 mph.

After dark, we checked in at the Ramada Inn in Blythe, California. I believe we ate in our rooms because we had all of the food and supplies from the motor home.

It was Christmas Eve. We had come through the mountains safely just minutes before the axle broke. Laurabelle had brought along a tiny, lighted Christmas tree. As we talked and sang, we knew that all was right with the world.   ❈

Silence Is Golden

The first of our many vacation trips to Hawaii was about 1975. Laurabelle and I took advantage of a real estate association charter of just $116 round trip on a DC-8 from Chicago O'Hare to Honolulu. Almost cost more than that to stay at home. No seat assignments. Box lunches. Just plain transportation.

We checked into the new Waikiki Beachcomber Hotel right across the beach from the grand old Royal Hawaiian Hotel whose spacious park-like front yard was still just that—a front yard of gardens. Flowers everywhere!

On Sunday morning, we awakened at some awful hour because of the five-hour jet lag. Our rooms were on the top, the tenth floor. Friends and associates with whom we were traveling had agreed to meet at 9:00 A.M. in the hotel lobby and then go out to breakfast at the Royal Surf Room in the Royal Hawaiian.

There were six elevators. One was being used for baggage. When an elevator was full, another gentleman and I stepped back and waited for another elevator. Coincidentally, the other man and I were dressed alike. Camel-hair jackets, brown trousers, cream-colored sport shirts, and white beach (golfer's) caps. All seemed right with the world, but wait!

> It was one of those days when my mother would have said, "Silence is golden."

We finally stepped into an elevator. The doors closed, and the bottom fell out of our little world. The elevator car was in free fall! It felt like our feet were five feet off the floor. Finally something automatically stopped our fall, and we gradually came to a jolting stop.

Now what? Well, a red light came on. A telephone was in a little glass-domed cabinet. Best of all, the world's loudest alarm bell was screaming like a sophomore at a ball game.

Now, it is quiet. The red light is glowing. The dust is settling. The phone is dangling on its cord. Here goes nothing.

My co-passenger on the thrill ride identified himself as an Oklahoma rancher. His wife was waiting in the lobby. I said, "Mine, too. Well, let's try the phone."

Suddenly, the phone came alive and a charming little girl voice called, "Are you there?"

I answered, "Where could we go?"

She did not like that answer. She said, "The elevator is stuck."

My happy rejoinder was, "Where?"

She said, "I think it is near the third floor."

My Oklahoma rancher was becoming very agitated. "My wife will kill me if someone can't convince her of where I am! She doesn't trust me out of her sight!"

We decided to try "the voice" again. This time she had some news: "The repairman is coming."

"When?"

"One hour," she said.

She didn't like it when I asked, "Where is he coming from? The mainland?"

She hung up.

"Okay," I said to my fellow adventurer. "Let's get out of here."

We took off our jackets and carefully came to a small area where the inside doors did not quite meet. We gradually worked our fingers into the crack, and we slid open the door about two feet. "Now," I said, "You unleash that 'dog' and latch spring. I will open the outside doors."

It wasn't easy, but we got it. Now we had both doors open about two feet or more. I braced myself. Oklahoma tossed our jackets to the floor about five feet below us. Then he hopped to the floor and braced himself in the gap. It was scary because I had to avoid dropping into the open shaft. I made it!

"Well, we thought it was over, but just wait. We went over to the fire doors and down the stairs to the lobby escalator. Whew! Suddenly, a little blonde lady came caterwauling across the lobby screaming, "Where's the woman *this* time?"

Apparently the Oklahoma rancher had not been kidding when he had earlier talked about his wife not trusting him. "Look," he said pointing to me, "we were stuck in the elevator. We just now got out."

As she continued to berate him, she grabbed him by the arm, headed to the lobby as she yelled for all to hear: "He's a big liar, too."

Dropping seven floors in the elevator was a scary thrill, but meeting that blonde bombshell was something else! We later encountered them laughing and smiling at each other. Apparently she got mad and then got glad again.

At least the elevator stopped at the *third* floor. Twelve hours later, that particular elevator was still posted, "Out of Service."

I remember the elevator ride, but I also remember that blond wildcat. By the way, I never said one word to them. I just smiled, joined our foursome, and got out of the way. It was one of those days when my mother would have said, "Silence is golden." ❊

Fourth of July
Church Sunday School Picnic

First, close the gates that hold the Holstein cows in the barn lot. Second, take a team and wagon, and a couple of men with flat shovels out to the beautiful oak grove.

"Why?"

To pick up the cow pies, of course!

Third, repair the door on the privy, pick up brush and limbs, and pile them on the permanent trash and brush pile. Fourth, help the men from the Church of the Brethren in town bring out to the oak woods the folding communion tables and folding chairs from the church, and set them all up as directed by John Erb. Brother Erb was the host who let us use his woods.

What was all this about? The picnic. The picnic!

The ingredients—250 Brethren people; a hot 4th of July day; a long, dusty lane; raucous, disturbed crows; long, white tablecloths; milk cans with water from the Erbs' well for iced tea, lemonade, and coffee; firewood; a fire pit; and some old tarpaulins from the Erb tool shed.

What now? People?

Among the early comers were the Netzleys in a new 1934 Chrysler Airflow with dealer plates and a C. C. Netzley logo.

Before long, at about noon, things were really shaping up. Young men with yardsticks donated by Beidelman Funeral Parlor were directing parking; other men had scythes and were cutting the bull thistles on the grounds. Ball, bats, gloves, and bases came out of someone's car trunk. Horseshoe pits were dug, and the stakes were driven in with ringing blows of sledgehammers. Most importantly of all, the food was being set out on

> **All seemed so right with the world at a church picnic!**

the long tables.

By 12:30, about 250 or so people thronged the woods, and it was time to pray and get down to the serious business of eating. The preacher called to folks to gather round and be quiet, please. He briefly prayed, and the food line formed in a hurry.

Flies! Big, black flies! Flies by the thousands left the cattle yard and barnyard and gave the picnickers their undivided attention. But the troops were ready—ladies and girls stood back of the serving tables and flapped dishtowels to shoo away the flies. (The modern-day EPA can yelp all they like, but I vote for good, strong fly spray!)

Food! Food! Food and some more food! Then ten gallons of homemade ice cream with plenty of strawberries, nuts, and chocolate syrup. Wonderful!

Now all the ladies worked at packing up the leftover food, and some men restocked the milk cans with iced tea, lemonade, and water.

It was time for the annual ball game. Married men against the single men. Eleven-inch softball.

Ten players to a side. This was about the time that short infielders were added to the lineup. The unmarried guys usually won. Those muscle-bound farmers, surprisingly, were not very good batters. I was a lousy fielder, but I could really hit!

The nuisance-age boys were busy and took time off now and then to harass any couples found in the back seat of any car. The ice cream was finished off. The tables and chairs were loaded. The trash was burned merrily in one of the horseshoe pits.

The cow herd was moving. They wanted to get back into the pasture. Farmers in attendance were ready to go back home and do the evening chores. The carloads of sun-burnt folks were ready to go back down the lane and head for home.

Another Church of the Brethren Fourth of July picnic was drawing to a close. All seemed right with the world!   ❋

BOYS' GLEE CLUB

Music and Melodies

Music is the universal language of mankind.
–Henry Wadsworth Longfellow

Men Singing

They came...from the great northlands of Europe...from the vast Orient...from the incredible tropical Africa...from the deserts of the East...from the length and breadth of Europe...from our southern neighbors. They came from the vast Pacific ...and as they came, it was ever the same—as men singing.

They came singing the tavern songs and the marches of England. Wild melodies of the Schottische and Cossack songs. They sang the sentimental ballads of the Latin countries. The distinct sounds of the Dark Continent. The rollicking Irish jigs. The work chants of China. They sang the marching songs and sentimental ballads of the Germanic nations...yes...as they came, it was ever the same—as men singing.

They built canals, roads, railroads, bridges, and steel mills. They settled the vastness of America, and, yes, as they built and settled upon this land...it was as men singing. They sang the songs of the Puritans, the Navy men, and the *couer-du-bois*...the sound of Africa by way of the rich music of the deep South...the great church music...the classical expression and the operatic product of the generations of great European composers.

Intertwined and inextricably entangled with the songs of the people came the songs of war.

In the audience tonight and in most audiences in this land since our beginnings...many of those present have served in the military and fought in war.

And they went to war, singing..."Yankee Doodle"..."Tenting Tonight"..."Long Way to Tipperary"..."A Rose That Grows in Flanders Field"..."Lili Marlene"..."A Nightingale Sang in Berkeley Square"..."We'll Meet Again"and "God Bless America..." and on

---

Men singing! Singing across the world... singing of their homes and lands... singing as they traveled along... singing as they built and toiled... men singing.

and on and again and again, men sang as they left loved ones, sang as they fought, sang as they came home—leaving behind white crosses and innocence and bringing home memories and pride.

What I say here is meant to make us more keenly aware of the roots of our wonderful heritage of song.

Across the sweeping panorama of time, *deeds* are recalled, *challenges* grasped, and *new understandings* mature and become history. Through it all, as the workman toils, as the soldier marches to war, as songs of worship touch men's hearts, as the fading bugle on a distant parade ground sounds that last retreat—comes ever the sound of men singing…men singing…men singing…   ❈

Naperville Men's Glee Club

In the winter of 1987–1988, I met Bonnie Klee. I was in attendance as a member of the Naperville Community Chorus. There were only two or three tenors present. A very attractive young lady with expressive eyes and long, dark hair moved from the soprano section, sat down beside me, and asked, "Mind if I sing tenor with you?"

I happily said, "Not at all," and she proceeded to do just that. It became apparent that she was an accomplished vocalist.

At the close of the rehearsal, we stood and she said, "I enjoyed singing with you."

I responded by saying something like, "The pleasure is mine."

I looked at this smiling lady and asked, "Are you also a director?"

She laughed and said, "Yes, I am."

An animated discussion ensued during which she told about her dream of forming and directing a men's glee club. She was really yearning for such an opportunity, and it showed.

All of this happened in only a few minutes of conversation at which point I asked, "Do you have an accompanist lined up?"

She laughed and said, "Yes."

I made up my mind! "You get your accompanist. I will recruit a basic small group, arrange for a practice hall, and see to it that we have a little money. Also…" and by this time, her eyes were sparkling and open wide, "I will contact Genevieve Towsley of the *Naperville Sun* and enlist her support."

Some time later, the details seemed to be worked out, and my son Alan and I told Bonnie at the Last Fling celebration, "Let's go!"

Genevieve had more than a passing interest. Her husband, Myron

> If only I have imparted some sense of the miraculous birth and growth of the Naperville Men's Glee Club.

Towsley, had sung in the old YMCA Male Chorus for many years.

About 1939 or 1940, Russ Witte, Bob Stauffer, Merlin Auner, and I enjoyed great exposure and popularity as a male quartet. We sang everywhere. We were organized and trained by E. A. "Art" Hill, Director of Music at Naperville High School. Myron Towsley's sister, Grace Fredenhagen, directed the YMCA Chorus. She and Art Hill had drafted the male quartet. The YMCA Chorus had about 30 members. They sang a couple of major concerts each year at Pfeiffer Hall. The hall was filled. We were very good!

At the very first rehearsal which we attended, Grace assigned me to the tenor solo in "Serenade" from "The Student Prince." I was not really that good, and I was "scared out of my wits."

I worried about that solo all year. I just knew I would flub it somehow. Well, to make a long story short, I did not flub it—I did well. Grace literally carried me on her baton. The memory grows dim, but I will never forget the wonderful support those chorus members afforded me. When I close my eyes and think back, I can still hear, "Overhead the moon is beaming, White as blossoms on the bough..."

Genevieve Towsley, with her marvelously unerring memory and appreciation of fine musical performances, had not forgotten the "Y" Chorus, her husband Myron's involvement, and the amazing talents of her sister-in-law, Grace Fredenhagen.

Remembering this and more, she included in her weekly column, a well-written announcement of the first rehearsal of the Naperville Men's Glee Club. Bonnie had laid out "Steal Away," "Cantique de Jean Racine," and "Sanctus" and hoped that a few men would come to the rehearsal hall at the Church of the Brethren. *Twenty-two men came!* We were off and running!

Five years have gone by. Many changes have occurred. Many events have transpired to the group and to its various members. There are, however, some wonderful constancies—the well-deserved and absolute respect of the Glee Club members, Bonnie's marvelously frank and insightful approach without ever being condescending or hurtful, her incredible talent along with an innate sense of when and how best to use that talent—I could carry on at some length in this vein. Rather, I think I shall only say that her love for the Glee Club shows through.

When one writes briefly, much is omitted. Perhaps in reminiscing, brevity is not bad if only I have imparted some sense of the miraculous birth and growth of the Naperville Men's Glee Club.   ✻

The Naperville Glee Club

> *When I was a young child, growing up in the Church of the Brethren in my hometown in Illinois, there was a certain man in the church choir who had a GOLDEN tenor voice. He loved to sing "In the Garden," and did so at least a couple times a year. I would sit in the pew, and when he sang, my heart just melted to the core. Little did I know that the Lord was preparing me for an eventual relationship with Him in my life.*   *–Michael Landis*

(Written to John Fry on July 19, 1999)

Moody and Sankey

About the time of the Chicago fire, Dwight L. Moody, who was not a musician, became more and more convinced that he needed music at his services.

While preaching in Indiana, he met and heard a singer named Ira Sankey. He knew that he had found his man. He wrote to Sankey.

However, Sankey was not really available. He hated traveling. He had a wife and three children. He had a good job as a tax accountant and auditor. He did not want to accede to Moody's request.

As Sankey sang, the crowd stilled.

Moody wrote yet again voicing an impassioned plea saying, "Sankey, I need you!' Finally Sankey came.

Come now to a typical evangelistic service. Large tents were often used but were subject to the vagaries of wind and weather. The real answer was the tabernacle!

Tabernacles of the middle to late 1800's were huge, temporary wooden structures. The sides were open, but canvas side curtains were often used. Depending on location as well as on the point in the century, lighting was by gas, carbide, or electricity. In any event, a tabernacle was rather primitive. Wooden benches by the hundreds; sawdust on the ground; a large, raised platform; and often a big megaphone on a sounding board afforded space for crowds of thousands of people.

Now, the noisy chatting crowd are finding seats. Folks are finishing their lunches or using the necessary tents or building as the stage hands carry in the harmonium, a small, reed organ with foot-operated air pedals.

Soon the lights are adjusted, and the platform man (or preacher) is seated behind the pulpit or table. A tall, bald, rather ungainly man walks across the stage and, sweeping back his coattails, seats himself at the harmonium, throws back his head, and, in a powerful, compelling, winsome voice begins to sing the songs of grace, love, intercession, hunger, love of God, and yearning for hope and happiness.

As Sankey sings, the crowd stills. A quiet expectancy fills the tabernacle, and as the last note of "I'm Praying for You" settles on the crowd, Moody, moved by the music, eyes filled with tears, strides onto the platform and begins to speak of Jesus and God's love.   ✽

Music Speaks

Music speaks at many times, in many places, and of many things.

Wherever we go…wherever we are…all through life…in our highs and in our lows…in our joys and in our woes…music speaks.

Music brings the songs of laughter: "Makin' Whoopee," "Ragtime Cowboy Joe," "Bei Mir Bist Du Schoen," "Three Iddie Fitties," "Toot Toot Tootsie Goodbye," "Homecoming Queen's Got a Gun"— "Homecoming Queen's Got a Gun"?!

Music speaks in a baby's first cry, in childhood song, in schooldays remembered, in campus songs, in the glad peal of wedding bells, in the beat of marching drums, and then in the whispered last, "I love you."

Music speaks to the heartstrings of all: "Silent Night," "Leaning on the Everlasting Arms," "The Stars and Stripes Forever," "Amazing Grace"—to the whole wonderful galaxy of human emotions.

> Music flings high the challenge to deeds and accomplishments.

Music says, "I love you"—"Truly"…"Forever"…"Always" and "Until"—one cannot count the ways.

Music bolsters the foundation stones of faith: "O Lord My God," "Abide with Me," "The Lord Is My Shepherd," "Rock of Ages"…

Music flings high the challenge to deeds and accomplishments…the call of the bugle…the hymns of the evangelicals…the cadence count and the marching feet…

Yes, music speaks of times and places…in joy and in sorrow…throughout lifetimes…to love and emotion…inspires and builds…and…

Finally, music speaks in farewells—not of goodbyes, but of promised reunions: "So Long," "Until We Meet Again," "Aloha," "Auf Wiedersehen," "We'll Meet Again," and so tonight, music speaks in this place until our farewell in song says, "I'll Be Seeing You." ✱

Amateur Hour

In 1932, radio was rapidly entering upon its early golden years. The days of theater organ music, banjo pickin', and the endless playing of early 78 rpm records were drawing to a close. The days of the news, political reporting, live shows such as "Amos and Andy," and the stories of the great depression were upon us. The best was yet to come.

Where else was anything going on?

A portly Hoosier with mellifluous voice calling himself Major Bowes brought us his amateur hour. Fantastic! Amateur musicians of all ages and backgrounds performed on nationwide radio. The Major had a huge gong. If a performer stumbled too badly or failed to get applause, the Major whacked the gong, and the aspiring artist was finished! If, however, a performer did well and the applause was thunderous, his or her success in the entertainment world was likely.

It was not long before local organizations and groups of many kinds began to sponsor and present "Amateur Hour" shows. These had several things in common. They paid cash prizes. The performers were known locally. Public address systems called loudspeakers were becoming available. After all, where else was anything going on? ✻

Nickel Dance

I will never forget "Blue Moon."

While in seventh grade at Ellsworth School, Bob Piper organized a band. There were ten players. I played the trombone.

Immediately after we had organized, Bob's sister Betty hired us to play for a Nickel Dance at the high school.

We had rehearsed one number to play at the dance. It was "Blue Moon," a currently popular ballad with a very danceable fox trot tempo and beat.

So! We showed up. We set up. We played. That's right—we played "Blue Moon" for the entire hour and a half dance.

We received a total pay of $2.00, and we were quite happy. We used the money to buy more music—to expand our repertoire! (Sheet music cost ten cents a copy in those days!)   ✽

Onward, Christian Soldiers!

I enrolled at North Central College in September of 1940. I was not strongly motivated. We were still in the depression. There were no jobs for high school graduates, certainly none for college graduates. So for $200 per semester, I enrolled in N.C.C.

You cannot truly experience college life while living at home. However, there were some fringe benefits that made the whole situation worthwhile. One of these benefits was singing in the choir at the First Presbyterian Church in Wheaton, Illinois.

For several years, the church had hired a male quartet and a mixed quartet to bolster their choir. The mixed quartet was from the American Conservatory of Music in Chicago. The members of our male quartet were recruited from North Central. The organist, Bob Hieber, also came from N.C.C.

The church building was a big, old, white frame high structure built, I am sure, about 1860. It seated about 450 persons. It sat on a corner just southeast of the park, and the church parsonage or manse was across a drive to the east.

The minister, Robert Graham Stuart, was a dark-haired, slender bachelor in his forties. He drove a huge Packard Phaeton automobile, rode a bicycle around town, and owned an Irish wolfhound. Folks referred to him as a modern-day ascetic. He was in charge.

In the short time we sang there, about two years, it seemed as though many things happened. A new $32,000 Evans pipe organ was installed. A pair of ancient columns from a temple in the Mediterranean were erected, flanking the antiphonal choir pews. (Boy, were they ugly!)

A little about personalities.

Our director, Mr. Roberts, was either the principal at Wheaton High School or the superintendent of Wheaton Public Schools. He was a man in his fifties, congenial, ambitious, well-trained in choral music, and he "wore well." We sang all music about 50 percent faster than any composer had intended. (Pause, if you will, to consider "Silent Night" sung in march tempo!)

Mr. and Mrs. Ward were two older faithful members. They, like the rest of the choir, were very good musicians.

At Christmastime, the choir, including the hired people, was invited to the Ward's home in Wheaton for a party. What a place! The main parlor was about half the size of a basketball court. Dozens of major pieces of furniture in conversational arrangements did not seem crowded. The fireplace was walk-in size. In later years, this home was to become a part of a complex of buildings occupied by an academy-type boys' school. Diverse personalities gave the choir a rather cosmopolitan air.

> Diverse personalities gave the choir a rather cosmopolitan air!

Most choir singers have heard or have sung "Seek Ye the Lord," but never have you really heard it until you sat entranced as Sam Scarborough stood out and filled the sanctuary with his pure, crystalline tenor voice. He got off pitch a lot, but one can't have everything! He was the tenor in the quartet from the Conservatory.

Ever hear an easy-flowing, rumbling-way-down-there bass? We had one! Rollie Ferch, a tall, handsome, tea-drinking seminarian was surely such a bass. Larry Bernhart followed Rollie in the job in our second year. He wasn't very big, but he had a big booming voice. Carlyle "Ky" Brand and I filled the job as tenors. He was a true first tenor. I was a good second tenor singing first.

We got pretty well acquainted with the lanky southern Wheaton college student who ran the lunch counter. He looked forward to seeing us pull up and park in my mother's 1936 Plymouth every Sunday morning.

Raisin toast at 15 cents and coffee at 10 cents were standard fare at the Walgreen's Drug Store in downtown Wheaton about two blocks from the church. In those days, all Walgreen's had busy lunch counters.

The McCormick family had long had substantial real estate holdings south of Wheaton. At one time this land was served by the C. A. & E.

Electric Railroad. Chauncey McCormick was in regular attendance at First Presbyterian. He and the members of his family sat on the left side about seven or eight rows from the front. He dressed for church—top hat, bow tie, starched collar, vest, striped trousers, and black tails. I cannot remember if he wore spats. I do recall that he wore a watch chain. When the hour approached a certain time, out came that watch, and the Reverend Robert James Stuart stopped preaching—right then!

I must mention that these Scotch Presbyterians operated with a certain elan that I much admired.

> **These Scotch Presbyterians operated with a certain elan that I much admired!**

Many years ago, an older, bushy-browed man, with mutton-leg sideburns, large nose and hoarse voice spoke vigorously, saying, "Leddie, look at a successful large business, and you will find a 'Scutsman in chairge.' " You know, maybe just maybe—he might be right!

I have saved the best for last!

We processed every Sunday. It was quite exciting. First of all, the old church was always full, standing room only. We robed in a parlor-like area behind the pulpit and choir loft. All of the robes were, of course, in good taste and very colorful.

We lined up in order and awaited the signal. As the organ pealed the opening bars of "Onward, Christian Soldiers," and with the congregation standing, the acolytes stepped out, carrying the Christian flag and the American flag. The flags were near parade size. Reverend Stuart, the pastor, and Erwin Soukup, the reader, followed.

We processed in strict march time to the peal of the great organ and the metronome-like sound of the wonderful bass sections. By the time we got to the back corner and turned toward the center aisle, the whole choir was in formation. The acolytes raised the flagstaffs high. Now we were really ready!

As the acolytes turned on the center aisle, the full organ burst forth, and the church began to bounce as the choir and congregation came to full voice: "Like a mighty army moves the church of God..."

Onward, then, ye people, Join our happy throng,

Blend with ours your voices In the triumph song;
Glory, laud, and honor, unto Christ the King:
This thro' countless ages men and angels sing.

Onward, Christian soldiers,
Marching as to war…

Down the aisle in continuing, stately march time, we brought our whole world to a peak of wonderful, joyful celebration! The last verse was sung as the choir entered their pews. While the music came to its thrilling climax and then came to a breathless ending, Rev. Stuart stepped forward and intoned: "*…Thou shalt love the Lord thy God with all thy heart, and with all thy soul, and with all thy mind. This is the first and great commandment. And the second is like unto it, Thou shalt love thy neighbour as thyself. On these two commandments hang all the law and the prophets.*" (Matthew 22:37–40)The choir then sang the call to worship.

We were seated. The mood was set. We all belonged.

The service which followed was reassuring and memorable—always!

A Piano

Laurabelle and I built a new home on Eagle Street in Naperville in 1949 and 1950. Actually, for a lack of funds, it was a few years before every last thing, including the garage was really finished.

I was working for the Metropolitan Life Insurance Company. In the course of my work, I made a service call on a family on the west side of Naperville near the Voss Brothers neighborhood store.

As I went through her life insurance policies, I could not help noting a beautiful, full-size spinet piano. I made an admiring comment about the piano.

She promptly asked, "Would you like to buy it?"

As the situation unfolded, she told me she had purchased the piano for her daughter a year earlier. Her daughter absolutely would not practice!

She said, "I paid over $600 for it, and you can have it for $300."

> That girl sat on the piano bench and wonderingly placed her hands on the piano.

She then went to say, "You can pay me from time to time as you have the money.

As it turned out, I did not have to avail myself of her kind offer, but I did buy the piano.

The north wall of the living room in our small new home was the space for a piano—someday.

Now I had the piano bought. How could I sneak it into the house and surprise Laurabelle? Brother Jim's wife, Mary Ellen, came to the rescue. She had a new baby and so had an adequate excuse to ask Laurabelle to come to her house and help with the laundry and cleaning. I told her I needed an hour and a half to get the piano in place before Laurabelle got home.

There were four of us—Herb Williams and myself, but I cannot remember who else helped. We hitched the utility trailer to the car, loaded a couple of planks, and went after the piano. Boy, was it heavy!

Back home, we backed up the trailer to the terrace steps, removed a door, laid the planks in place, wrestled the piano inside, picked up the planks, rehung the door, and—you guessed it—here came Laurabelle around the corner in the big green Packard Clipper, just as I drove the car and trailer back down the front yard walk and over the curb to the street.

Laurabelle parked in the drive. She really looked puzzled.

As I caught up to her at the door, she stepped inside, stopped, and exclaimed, "A PIANO!"

The lovely girl laughed and cried as she stood there completely surprised. Then she sat on the piano bench and wonderingly placed her hands on the piano.

That girl sat there laughing and crying for at least ten minutes.

All of this time, she exclaimed again and yet again—"A PIANO!" ✻

Praetorius at Forest Junction

The North Central College Men's Octette was coached and trained from February through May by Professor C. C. Pinney. In early June, they "hit" the road—eight men, an accompanist, Director Pinney, two new Plymouth cars, and a trailer for luggage.

We traveled and sang all summer. At the end of the first ten days, Prof returned to campus, and we nine were on our own. We presented 132 concerts in 83 days.

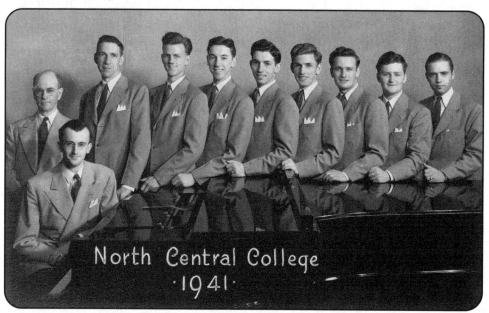

The North Central College Octette
I, John Fry, am the second from the right.

We sang a full second concert on a Sunday morning. We then loaded up and headed for a church camp at Forest Junction, Wisconsin. Cottages, a dining hall, washrooms, a playing field, some private summer cottages and, of course, a tabernacle were sort of crowded together in a wooded setting.

We sang several numbers and then, soaked with sweat, sat down on the front bench to hear the bishop. We heard him all right. This big, dark-complexioned, black-haired, black-suit-clad, medium-sized giant of a man plunged across the platform, arrived flat-handed at the crude wooden pulpit and thundered, "He ran! Yes,…he ran to tell Jesus…"

I do not remember the sermon.

I do remember what almost happened. I almost ran to become a preacher and to tell the world about Jesus. Somehow, it never happened.

I wonder!   ❈

There Is Always Music

The music goes round and round. "Three Little Fifties." "Bei Mïr Bist Du Schoen." "Ragtime." "Cowboy Joe" and again on and on and on.

All the while, as the rolling thunder of World War II crept over the horizon the music of Glenn Miller, Glenn Gray, Blue Barron, and many others interwove the tapestry of the sound of the big band era. Soon, "Moonlight Serenade," "In the Mood," "American Patrol March," and swing tunes galore carried us right on into and through the convulsive times of war and dumped us into the turbulent fifties and sixties right on until now.

Elvis, The Beatles, The Everly Brothers, Jan and Dean, Beach Boys, Richie Valens, The "Big Bopper," Bill Haley and the Comets, and again, name after name, group after group, and songs, songs, songs, and on and on…and at the same time, through it all, there is always music.   ❋

There's Something About a Band

Central Park in Naperville, Illinois. 7:30 P.M. July 2, 1998. The square block of lawns is full of happy people. In fact, a couple of thousand latecomers are moving into every possible space on adjoining streets and parkways. The refreshment gazebo is well-stocked with pies and cakes, cookies, ice cream, various kinds of soft drinks, and, of course, coffee.

The 100 members of the Naperville Municipal Band are filling the brightly lighted band shell and are beginning to warm up as they take their places. Held in reserve in the left wing waiting to be called are 36 members of the Naperville Men's Glee Club. They will join the band at several points in the concert.

Kids are climbing the War of 1812 cannon and sliding off. The trash barrels are filling fast as the picnickers "pick up." The batteries of cannon are forming up and clearing the field of fire. In appropriate uniforms with proper equipment, they reenact the firing of cannons from the various wars from 1778 until 1865. What a colorful group they form in all.

Church bells across the street begin to toll the hour, and as it strikes eight times, the band breaks into its theme song version of "Strike Up the Band." As the last score rings out, the drums begin to roll; and Director Ron Keller enters briskly stage front. He raises his baton and directs the band and the audience; 8,000 voices join in singing "The Star-Spangled Banner." The Glee Club exits, and the wonderful music and songs of barracks and battles begins the concert.

Meanwhile, back by the old cannon, just before the music begins, there is a story to be told. John Fry heard Ed Kraisinger say, "Of the pies ever made, I like coconut cream the best." John slipped away and worked his way through the crowd to where the ice cream social was being held at the gazebo. Once he worked his way up to the counter, he looked in vain for coconut cream pie.

A young woman noticed his crestfallen expression and asked, "John, may I help you?"

"I am looking for a piece of coconut pie," John said.

She laughed delightedly, reached under the counter, and brought out a large pie-carrying dish and said, "Ask, and you shall receive."

She cut that huge beautiful, beautiful pie in only six pieces. The pie stood tall and firm as she said, "It looks just perfect."

It was!! John thanked her profusely and began to make his way back to where Ed and his family were seated. When he saw me turn toward him, he looked puzzled. When he saw that glorious piece of pie, he just sort of smiled and said, "Oh, John!"

I am quite sure that whenever Kraisinger and Fry meet, he is saying to himself, "Oh, John!"   ✳

Recollections

We must always have old memories
and young hopes.
–Arsène Houssaye

The Graveyard

It was on high ground right behind the church. It was stock-free fencing. It had two woven wire steel-framed fence gates. One gate led into the Indian side of the graveyard, and the other led across into the white folks' side. The brown grass and weeds were sparse. The stone markers were modest, weatherbeaten, and, for the most part, slightly crooked. I do not recall any shrubs or trees.

But why did I want to weep?

Most of the markers on the Indian side told of babies or small children. But, why did I want to weep?

It wasn't the iron-grey sky. It was not the graves of so many children, nor was it the gentle soughing of the breeze in the nearby cottonwood break. No, none of these.

It was the gifts. The graves of the children were all decorated and marked. Some slept alone except for a single toy or doll. Many felt the nearness of a simple bouquet. Most graves had little tin cars or trucks, with an occasional ball or some marbles in a jar—simple gifts. Yes, it was the gifts that brought the tears. For you see, they were all things that could still be played with and used.

My heart asked as I realized that they and their loved ones had not heard, had not seen, and did not understand that the lovely little ones were held in God's arms.

They were not here. Toys would not reach them. I concede the happy gift of a family and close loved ones. All this I confess. But as the tears slowly dry, I ask again and again, "Had they not seen? Don't they know? Have they not heard?"

Surely they should have known that God gathers them in His arms and takes them Home to Himself. Surely they could have been told as the story came down through the years, *"Come unto me…"*

I reconsider the scene and my saddened heart, saying. "It must be that they have never come to trust Him. They are so simple and so uneducated. Thank heavens, I have not seen this elsewhere." But wait just a time.

The grey sky was now gathering the last remaining life and colors of the distant prairie sunset. The shadows had begun to lengthen, and I returned to the old church. I wish I could have said to those still here, "They are not here! They have joined their Heavenly Father. Have faith. Have faith. Have faith."   ✽

I Love a Parade!

"I love a parade," and the first one I remember is the Naperville Centennial Parade in 1931, and I remember it well! At that time, the population of Naperville was fewer than 5,000 people.

Naperville was blessed with a YMCA; Northwestern College (renamed North Central College); Evangelical Theological Seminary; Nichols Library (municipal); the services of the Chicago, Burlington, and Quincy Railroad (CB&Q); Kroehler Manufacturing Company (for many years the world's largest manufacturer of upholstered furniture); a host of active churches; and 12 saloons. In various ways, these institutions and their facilities were helped by the populace in planning and holding a BIG parade. It was truly a cosmopolitan effort.

I was nine years old when this granddaddy of all parades was held. The parade units utilized the entire Pilgrim addition subdivision area and exited onto Washington Street.

The Centennial theme was well presented by theme floats and marching units. I recalled reading later that the parade was four miles long! That was enough to imprint indelibly the events of the day on me as a nine-year-old. There were hundreds of horses, several hundred floats, and bands, bands, and more bands.

The veterans of World War I were much in evidence. After all, the great war to end all wars had ended only 13 years earlier. Veterans of the Spanish-American War with their distinctive campaign hats were much in evidence also. I was not impressed, however, by the Grand Army of the Republic (GAR). Here they came! Some marching. Some riding in open cars. I think also there may have some veterans of the Civil War who rode in buggies. I don't think any rode horseback. After all, they were more than 80 years old.

Oh, yes! The drums! The whole parade marched to the mile-eating, rattling tempo of the shallow snare drums. A-rat-a-tat-tat-a-rat-a-tat-tat. The simple beat never wavered—a-rat-a-tat-tat—I can't forget that sound…

But you know, the amazing thing about the Centennial parade was not the crowd of tens of thousands, nor the great pageant at the college field, not even the parade itself. No! The amazing thing is that it happened at all!

In 1931, we were still caught in the inexorable grip of the great rending economic Depression. Most people had very little cash money. Those who did have money virtually ruled the day.

Naperville had a *certain something!* As far as I know, that parade in 1931 surpassed any event held in the area for many years to come—in attendance and in interest.

Of course, it was different than the incredible series of events and doings promoted by Jack Kelly at the Century of Progress, commonly known as the Chicago World's Fair.   ✽

The Lightning Strike of 1972

Summertime. Late afternoon. Hot, sultry day. Storm approaching. Line of black clouds.

Several of our earthmoving crew and I stood in the open overhead door of our maintenance shop, talking and drinking coffee.

Can't get much closer!

Suddenly, like a crack of doom, a bolt of lightning struck a newly planted tree some 25 feet behind me. Two forks of electricity followed guy wires from the tree to fence posts and split the posts to smithereens, leaving them afire. A third bolt came across the drive and hit my left foot.

I was a mess—left boot smoked, hair refused to lie down, terrible headache, sulphur smell everywhere—and all those guys laughing uproariously.

I was just really mad because I had been drenched by my spilled hot coffee!

Can't get much closer! ❊

Loose Rope

Along in the 1930's, a man named Lehnen and Clyde Savage, Sr., formed the DuPage Boiler Works. Clyde Savage was a short, peppery ball of fire who appeared to go at a frantic pace and lived as though there were no tomorrow.

Legend has it that at some point in the early days of the company, before or after the venture was organized, the boiler works people asked the bank to loan money for the venture. Apparently, the bank regarded Mr. Savage as a wild-stallion-riding entrepreneur, so they replied, "No loan."

The primary product of the boiler works was galvanized steel tanks for hot and cold water storage or heating. The company was located at the foot of East Chicago Avenue in a complex of buildings on land that was part of the old Ritzert gravel pit. The boilers were shipped by rail. The freight depot was on the north side of the railroad tracks between Center and Ellsworth Streets. The most direct route to the freight depot from the boiler works was by way of Columbia or Julian to Fifth Avenue and then west to Ellsworth.

Every working day for years and years the message was the same!

The boiler-works truck was a big, old brown flatbed with stake body and racks. The boilers were loaded standing on end. A three-quarter-inch rope or two were used to tie the load. The rope was always tied loosely.

Now, imagine *this* route to the depot. It ran on Chicago Avenue to Washington Street and then north on Washington to Fifth Avenue. In those depression years, the only traffic signal in downtown Naperville was at Washington and Jefferson. The man driving the truck had strict orders: lock the brake at the light, "rev" the engine, and "pop" the clutch when the light changes.

There are no words adequate to describe the ringing, clashing, crashing boiler tanks as they rocked back and forth at that stop. Guess what was on that crash-bang-clanging corner—that's right—the bank!

Every working day for years and years, the message was the same, "Listen, you bankers. There goes another load of DuPage Boiler Works tanks!"

That'll show 'em!   ❀

1931 Church Camp Revisited

I stand at the west windrow of cannibalized grain combines in a wooded grove at the edge of Franklin Grove, Illinois. This is the site of the old church campground. With my back to the sprawling farm tractor and farm machinery salvage yard, I pause.

I look toward the old swimming pool. All that remains are two concrete lampposts and some rubble. I can picture clearly the concrete pool, the fence, pop cooler, candy case, showers, and pool-side benches. In the early 1930's, the place was like a little bit of Heaven.

I drift along as the memories flood over me. There was the old tabernacle with the sawdust floor. Here was the ballfield. That's a backstop post! Right here by this, the only remaining dorm cottage, is where I stood to blow reveille and taps! The cabins marched up the hill right there! Here—here is the old dining hall. It's full of trash and farm machinery parts now, but that's no problem.

Cap in hand and barefoot as always, the boy stood on a dining room chair and began to sing.

I just close my eyes…close my eyes…and listen…

I can still hear the reason for "church camp revisited." It is not the traces of old buildings. It is not the memories of baseball, box hockey, rope making, and game-board making. Nor is it the singing in the tabernacle. And no, it isn't butterfly mounting or even fishing. Not even the pig roast!

It is the boy in the cemetery. All during camp week, we were aware of the boy in the large cemetery on the hill beside the campgrounds. A wire cattle fence enclosed it. A barefoot boy about ten years old was often seen there. He stood by the fence much of every day—just watching and listening.

As the week wore on, Reverend White, the director of the church camp group from Naperville, invited the boy over to watch the ball games and to mingle with the campers. The boy looked a little different. He couldn't speak quite normally. He seldom tried. His appearance was somewhat different. I can't remember just how.

Camp weeks ran from Sunday evening 'til Saturday noon. Friday afternoon came quickly. The boy from the cemetery was invited to supper. Camp meals were always great fun. We sang. Then we sang. Then we sang some more.

But this mealtime was different. Something happened. The barefoot boy asked if he could sing. Reverend White stood and called out, "Our young friend wants to sing for us. What are you going to sing, young man?" The boy did not answer. Cap in hand and barefoot as always, he stood on a dining room chair and began to sing in feathery, soft tones, "I come to the garden alone, while the dew is still…"

As he sang, all speech trouble was forgotten and gone. In a clear strong voice of unusual timbre and winsomeness, he sang several verses of the wonderful old hymn. By the last chorus, "And He walks with me, and He talks with me, and He tells me I am His own," a hush had long since settled over the dining hall.

I cannot recall who shared our cabin at camp. I do not remember how we got to Franklin Grove. I cannot come up with the name of the campground. I am not even sure of the exact year. But it does not matter!

It does not matter, because I do recall…I will ever remember…I shall never forget…that day when as the last phrase, "none other has ever known," faded away, the cemetery boy held me in the palm of his hand.

Isn't it amazing how God speaks to us at unexpected times, in ordinary places, and in many voices?   ✸

Meditation on Christmas Eve, 1988

Midpoint in Handel's incredible work, "The Messiah," an alto singer stands in silence. The simple accompaniment begins and leads her into the hauntingly lovely air, *He shall feed His flock…and gently lead those that are with young.*

How did the writer of Isaiah 35, and, in turn, Handel, the composer, catch the beauty and strength of those words? Surely it could have come only through experience. I, too, came to understand through homely experience.

The place:	Farm country, Kendall County, Illinois
The time:	Afternoon—sometime in January 1978
The event:	A farm auction sale

In a typical farm closing-out auction sale, the hayrack items, the household goods, the miscellaneous items, the farm implements, tractors, trucks, and combine have all in turn been sold. Now, on this terribly cold winter day in northern Illinois, it is time to sell the cattle. The family-raised herd of mixed beef cows, calves, steers, and the great Charolais bull will each in turn go to the highest bidder.

> **The old white-faced Hereford is old— in a word, she is beautiful!**

The buyers and onlookers casually and, out of long experience, form a loose circle in the cattle yard between the barn and the shed. Here we see the anxious 4-H'er hoping to buy a club calf to show a year hence at the County Fair. There, planted in front, cigar-clenched, cane in hand, eyes squinting into the late-in-the-day sun stands the heavy-set, older professional cattle buyer. Over yonder stands the newlyweds just started in farming. He tries to look calm while remembering his dad's admonition, "Decide what you will pay. Don't bid too slow. Don't go more than ten percent over your figure—**ever!**" His wife, mittened hands held close, is just too excited for words.

These, along with casual friends, other bidders, and onlookers quiet down as the auctioneer climbs over the gate, pulls hard on his Stetson, raises his voice and says, "All right folks, it's been a good sale so far. Now let's get in there and bid so the Missus won't be disappointed. She and Charlie raised all of this stock right here on the farm. All the cows and heifers have been tested." Turning aside, he asks in a loud voice, "George, do you have anything to say?"

The young man so addressed replies, "No, Bert. It's just like you said. Dad raised all of them right here on the farm except the bull. He's a four year old, and all the calves are from him."

Bert, the auctioneer, calls out, "All right boys, let's have the first cattle." A man opens the barn door and a bunch of six steer calves ranging in color from pale tan to reddish gold bolt into the man-formed ring. Bert begins his chant. "All right, boys. These are March calves. Selling 'em by the head. Take choice or all. Who'll gimme three hunnert? Three hunnert? Three hunnert? I got two. I got two. I want two and a quarter. I want two and a quarter. Now two hunnert, now two hunnert, now two hunnert, two-fifty? Make it two-seventy-five? Two-seventy-five? Two-seventy-five? All done? I'm going to the bank, two-seventy-five? Two-seventy-five? Sold two fifty—Tom—you want 'em all? Tom takes 'em all."

And so goes the sale. An hour has passed. Most of the cattle have been sold. Bert is hoarse. It is very cold. A couple more head and then the bull have yet to enter the ring, be auctioned, sold, and go through the swinging doors into the cattle shed. The barn door swings again, and an aged cow heavy with calf walks slowly into the ring.

She is old—a white-faced Hereford, from her pink nose to the wide, white, ringleted face; white fringed ears; beautiful, large eyes; huge, curled horns; heavy, russet-red coat to her white, broom-tail. She is, in a word, beautiful! She is also nervous! Who are all of these people? Her sides heave as the calf in her moves.

Bert takes up his chant again. "All right, folks, this old cow has calved every spring for 14 years. Just look at her! She is due to calve again in March. Bred to the Charolais bull. I want four hunnert. Yes! Four hunnert.

I got two-fifty. Mike?! Did you bid? Three hunnert? I got three hunnert, three hunnert, I want three-twenty-five."

The newlywed farm couple bid, "Three-hundred thirty!"

The old cattle buyer winks and Bert calls, "I got three-forty. I want three-fifty. Three-fifty?" He turns to the couple.

The young man gulps, clutches his wife's hand, and jumps the bid, calling out, "Three-eighty!"

Bert screams in well-played excitement. "I got three-eighty. Make it four hunnert. I got three-eighty; make it four hunnert. I'm gonna sell her. Four hunnert once, four hunnert twice. This is the last cow. Four hunnert? Four hunnert? Four hunnert? Sold at three-eighty!"

The crowd chuckles at the obvious delight of the young wife. But what about the cow? This babble of excited voices, cigar smoke, cold wind, and all of these strangers pressing near have her excited and confused. With head swinging from side to side, the worried cow lows and circles—seeking a place to go, a place to be led. Just then the new owner reaches out, takes her by the horn, and says softly and tenderly, "Come on, old girl." Her eyes turn limpid again. The lashing tail slows. She lows softly and goes quietly with her own new owner.

Now I don't have to wonder how the writer of Isaiah could write so beautifully. Now I don't have to ask how Handel was inspired to compose the hauntingly, lovely melody. For now, I too have seen how He reaches out and gently leads those that are with young.   ✳

A Plymouth Christmas

In December of 1942, we had been at war for one year. The home front was keenly aware of changes in their daily lives. Gasoline and tires were rationed, college enrollment was plummeting, and the familiar faces around Naperville were disappearing every week.

I was attending school part-time at North Central College and pumping gas evenings and Saturdays at Lee Nelson's Pure Oil Station in downtown Naperville at Van Buren and Washington. It was a true neighborhood service station. I could wash and chamois a car in about 20 minutes. A simple puncture repair of a 600 x 16 tire took less than 15 minutes. We greased cars, charged batteries, pumped gas, changed oil, installed mufflers, and cared for all the many problems to which cars of the era fell prey.

My destination– Plymouth, Michigan– and the girl!

By this time, we were enjoying a national highway speed limit of 35 miles per hour. Fortunately for all, the police forces had shrunk considerably, and night patrols were almost non-existent in country areas.

So it was that I planned to drive from Naperville to Plymouth after I closed the station at 6:00 P.M. My 1933 Plymouth coupe with a straight exhaust pipe, booted tires, and rumble seat full of gas cans and jug was ready to go. The temperature was 10° below zero, a cardboard on the radiator grill, a little rubber-bladed defroster fan whining valiantly, a red-eyed heater switch giving support to the song of the heater, ten gallons of ethyl gas, and four gallons of kerosene in the tank, and a blanket around my legs, off I went.

What a wonderful night. The pavement was dry. The fields were white. The moon was full. The engine was literally singing, and my heart was full to bursting with excitement at being on the way to Plymouth and Laurabelle!

What a trip. That little car rocketed through Niles, Jackson, Ann Arbor, and finally into Plymouth after midnight, having stopped only once for coffee and soup, and to pour some jugsful of gas into the tank. It was now 20° below zero, but I hardly knew or cared. I had driven 312 miles in six and one-half hours. All seemed right with the world!

Forty-seven years later, it seems like yesterday! ✽

Pneumonia—Twice

Car crazy? Wasn't everyone? Especially teenagers? My first car was a 1927 Hupmobile owned in partnership with my brother Bob. It got wrecked.

In the fall of '39, I paid an older man from Warrenville $32.50 for a straight, clean 1930 Ford Model A coupe.

It needed paint, tires, and a valve job. I accomplished all three and promptly came down with pneumonia.

Dr. Martin, bless his soul, prescribed Sulfathiazine. It was newly available. It didn't seem to work. He thought I was dying. I rode to St. Charles Hospital in nearby Aurora in a hearse-ambulance. Scary! I didn't die.

A neighbor, Mr. Cole, had tried to buy the Model A from me because he needed it on his farm in Indiana. He came to the hospital to try one more time. I relented. He paid me $140. I paid the hospital the $140. There went my Model A.

Close call?

————

In 1942, I tried twice to enlist in the Air Force. Both times I failed the physical because of a partial color perception. I learned later that guys got copies of the Kishashari color test and faked their way through the exam.

So, I just waited to be drafted. The day came. On February 3, 1943, I was inducted into the AOS at Fort Sheridan. A day later, we were shipped to Camp Grant.

Believe me, February is not a nice month in Rockford, Illinois, with 20° below zero in the daytime and 20° below zero at night. No boots. Mud and snow. Not enough sleep. Unheated barracks. Everybody coughing. Twenty percent of the company in the hospital.

Tough sergeant. Homesick. Feverish. Finally went on sick call. Sat down on a bench in the clinic. Awakened four days later in a hospital bed. Fever had broken. IV's removed. Fourteen pounds lighter. Back to the company and active duty. Never did recall any part of those four lost days.

Back I went to the company where they gave me two stripes and shipped me to Fort Benjamin Harrison in Indianapolis, Indiana, and technician's school.

Ha-Ha, pneumonia—you missed again!   ✜

Sometimes...

Sometimes...I agonize over mistakes recalled from long ago.

Sometimes...I marvel at what, in my lifetime, has been done.

Sometimes...I recall with terrible freshness the hurts of long ago.

Sometimes...I realize the strength of love in marriage.

Sometimes...I relive moving experiences with a clarity beyond expression.

Sometimes...I ask where the years have gone.

Sometimes...I feel God is right here with me.

Sometimes...I forget God as if *I* have all of the answers.

Sometimes...I find happy memories clearing my mind of all else.

Sometimes...I savor successes remembered.

Sometimes...I just can't face mistakes recalled.

Sometimes...I am lighthearted.

Sometimes...I live too much with anxiety.

Sometimes...I can't face how short of the mark I have fallen.

Sometimes...I now say, "So little time." ✽

Tell Me

Tell me it took God seven days to make the world.

Explain that the world evolved over millions of years.

Rationalize the wonderful tales of the Old Testament.

Argue the improbability of the miracles of Jesus.

Speak to me of modern-day miracles.

Be ever so disparaging of life in Christ.

It matters not, because I believe that God is able and present in all things. God is able to make the world in a week.

He, in His infinite patience, can let a world evolve in seven times seven millions of years.

The stories of the Old Testament are true because of their teachings and truths.

Miracles chronicling the footsteps of Christ bring the story of redemption and salvation.

How can anyone deny the possibility of modern miracles of health, sickness, and happenings?

Celebrate the promises of Christ—let the disparager and belittler fade to naught.

Yes! Tell, explain, rationalize, argue, and disparage; it matters not because God is able, infinite in patience, a teacher, a miracle worker, and when words and all else fail...God! ✽

The Tornado of October 1992

As the tornado roared over me, it picked up my truck and me, moved us a few feet, set us down, and plastered us with about an inch of mud! Then the rain poured, the wind renewed for a moment, and the truck was washed clean; the inside of the truck cab filled with a heavy, cold fog.

I said aloud, "After all I have been through, what a dumb way to die."

Well, I looked around. I saw that the big trees nearby had been twisted off about 15 feet above the ground. Through a break in the clouds, the sun began to appear. It looked like a giant had dumped trash and trees and limbs all over the area.

> **It looked like a giant had dumped trash and trees and limbs all over the area.**

The forerunner of all this is quite simple. I had been at Tamarack Golf Course, our project on Illinois Route 59. As I left the parking lot, a line of clouds to the west looked dangerous; and the warning sirens had begun to wail.

Soon I was going east on 104th Street—running away from the storm quite nicely. I knew I could turn south at Book Road and be well away on a divergent track. When I reached Book Road, lo and behold, there was a second small twister blocking my planned route. I turned north across the storm and gave her the devil. That's when it got me.

I suppose I will die of something someday…   ❋

Triple

Cold, clear, Naperville morning in November. Nice tracking snow. Second day of pheasant hunting.

Brother Bob, son Alan, and I. We drove into the yard at the Myers farm in the pickup. I cautioned the guys, "No noise. Don't slam the doors. Load the guns slowly and softly. Bob, you go around the big trees. Alan, come around the south end of the hedgerow. I'll take the middle. When you reach the corn stubble, be alert!"

It worked like a dream. As we moved into the fields, there were fresh tracks everywhere we looked. The pheasants were feeding exactly where I had hoped.

I called softly, "We are right on them." At that, six cock pheasants went up. We all shot in just a few seconds. Bob yelled, "I got a double." Alan called, "I got one." Bob was terribly excited. He had never gotten a double.

Without thinking, I said, "I got a triple." Bob did not believe me. He picked up two birds. Alan picked up one bird. I picked up two birds. Where was the sixth bird? Bob insisted that it did not exist.

I said, "Look—three empty shells—three birds."

Bob insisted, "You shot one twice and missed."

I said, "Bob, you *know* I do not miss."

The discussion was going nowhere, so I suggested, "Let's make one last big circle and see what we can find." We had almost completed the circle walk when a small hawk took off back behind where Alan had been when we shot. I walked over to where the hawk had flown, and of course, there was my third bird. The hawk had found it still warm and fresh. Bob was so upset that I wished I had not found the bird.

The explanation was simple. The pheasant had flushed behind Alan and me to my left. I had whirled and shot the cock from the hip, and then raised the gun as I swung back and shot the second and third pheasants. The problem had been that I had shot too fast to remember.

Well, as I said, I almost wished that I had not found the third pheasant. The thrill of Bob's first double was gone.

Over the years when Bob has been present, I have never mentioned my TRIPLE!   ❊

The Rifle

"Where did you get a new 1917 pattern Lee-Enfield 30-06 Army rifle?" I asked in amazement!

The handsome, young blonde university student answered, "We bought it at the armory in town yesterday for $35."

"Was it packed in cosmoline grease?"

"Yes. We used gasoline to clean it."

I had been brought to this point by the sound of a large bore rifle being fired. We were guests in a home near a little town in Oklahoma ranch country. I had come to sing at the wedding of a friend. In this country, cattle are counted by the thousands. Ten-thousand acre fields of wheat are common. There seemed to be a rifle in every truck. That part of the state is all red-clay prairie land.

> **There seemed to be a rifle in every truck.**

When I heard the flat sound of the Lee-Enfield, I stepped outside and thus came my question: "Where did you get a new 1917 pattern Lee-Enfield?" Now I queried, "What are you shooting at?"

His beautiful, blonde girlfriend pointed and said, "That pail on the fence post."

I looked hard and sure enough, about 2,000 feet across the shimmering wheat, there was a rusty five-gallon pail on a barbed wire fence post. "Would you like to shoot it?" she asked.

I bridled asking, "Do you have a sling? Does it kick?"

"We don't have a sling," the young man replied, "but it doesn't kick much."

"Well, okay. I'll try a shot." This was a real challenge. No sling, a light breeze moving across the billowing, nearly ripe wheat, and, of course, open sights. I held high about three feet and allowed for the wind and squeezed. The trigger was smooth as silk, and I clearly heard a round hit. But, did it hit the pail or the hard red soil?

There is no way to know when you are going to blurt out something silly. As we walked along the fence to the pail, I said, "You know, I believe I hit it low and to the left."

Low on the pail and just left of center it was! As we walked back, the young man (whose name I never learned) asked, "Would you like to try it again?"

"Oh, no," I said. "I don't want to get a sore shoulder from firing without a sling."

The wedding rehearsal was that evening at the church. The college crowd of 20 or 30 young people were standing together in the back of the church. Someone asked, "Why are the kids pointing at Mr. Fry?"

The rifle shot! How many rounds do you think I would have had to fire to hit that pail again?! One hundred?!   ❋

Walk or Hunt?

Even a mongrel pup can hunt cover. "Why can't you?" Such a question might well be asked of most modern upland game hunters. Yet, most hunters today don't know or have much conception of working a piece of ground. Most just walk along, waiting for the game to appear.

Have you ever watched a "walker" pick a clean corn row in a picked field and walk straight down the field, gun at the port? Of course you have!

Have you ever wondered why the teenage farm boy or the grizzled old timer gets game in all sorts of weather (and many times in the area you pronounced "hunted out")? Or have you ever felt frustrated and puzzled by the continued success of an acquaintance whose every hunt was successful in places where you rarely saw game?

When you get an opportunity to hunt with a successful hunter, watch him! Watch how he "sizes up" the area to be hunted and heads for certain spots. Are you aware that he has figured on wind direction and probable flight direction of game as well as the most likely cover?

I am writing primarily for the Midwestern small-game hunter whose major game opportunities are for cottontail rabbits, squirrels, and pheasants—in that order. Cottontail rabbits offer more hunters more opportunity for real hunting than any other upland small game. Seasons are longer, bag limits large, and rabbits plentiful. Rabbits almost invariably bed down after night-time foraging and running in an area somewhat apart, if possible, from their feeding, watering, and running area.

There are, of course, many exceptions. Brush-pile rabbits, wood- or junk-pile rabbits, and rabbits using abandoned chuck holes, tile, or culverts behave somewhat differently. Under such conditions, cottontails can also be hunted successfully without disturbing their nearly impregnable homes.

Here's how. Let the weather work for you. Always approach from downwind. Don't "charge" the area. Drift and wander into the periphery of the cover, watching well ahead.

On almost any unseasonably warm day, be it November, January, or July, cottontails will be sunning at the edge of cover, not usually out in the complete open, but in partial cover where the late afternoon sun slants in to warm them. They have slept all day, and now before the comparative safety of twilight, they are in the "family room" just loafing around, near cover.

So where do you hunt in mid-afternoon on a sunny January day? On the sunny side of hedgerows, heavy brush, fences known for chuckholes, old farm pits, orchards, or woodpiles. Work along upwind and at ten or fifteen yards from cover. The rabbits will be half asleep and will smell you or hear you long before they see you. If working upwind means looking into the sun or its reflection on snow, your distance from the cover will let you keep your head turned away from direct sun and its impairment of visual acuity.

Why so much caution and care? Because you are after game that during most of the season is "holed up." Bonus game!

Remember, you stay well away from cover and move in closer only when you think you see game or to examine cover that is heavy or unusually attractive. Why? Because game is so close to cover that when it moves you have to be at shotgun range and shoot *right now.* Also, you will be amazed at the number of cottontails you kick out from under foot. Nail them when they hit the edge of cover!

One might well ask, "What about all the game that 'sits tight'?" The answer is simple. Plan your hunt so that later you can move right back down the same cover close in. You will move rabbits you never see, miss many you do see, and get no shot at others. In other words, you will walk the fence after you have worked it. What if you had walked it first? These same areas of hedgerows, brush piles, farm pits, etc., can be hunted profitably at one other time. In an area reasonably free of foxes, a warm rainy day can be a real producer. Most of the cottontails will be in light fallen leaves, grass, or bull thistle cover and will streak for heavy cover only when you literally kick them out. Hunt open woodland in the same way.

Some cover is good always and at all times. Even a "walker" will get rabbits in a weedy field of picked corn. But usually a "hunter" can follow the "walker" and get more rabbits. Once again, here's how. Cottontails bed down facing the wind. You won't always know which way the wind was blowing during the night. Examine the nest or set of the first cottontail of the day. Then hunt his friends "face to face." In average cover as you drift back and forth, you should see about half the game before it moves. Don't forget to work grassy swales and low spots very carefully. If a field is not producing, try this trick. Stop every few minutes and look around. On a windy day, cottontails are not easily disturbed and may let you move on by if they think they are not observed. Backtracking and stopping to look around will move them as quickly as the noise and movement of your passage.

Soybeans and cottontails go together. Rabbits are always found in some numbers in the straw piles of bean stubble. Two factors determine how numerous they may be. First is the availability of nearby cover in snowy or wet weather and second, location of water in dry weather. Cottontails thrive on a dry, bulky diet and need water in good supply. Even a "walker" can get results here. But a hunter will get them more easily. One will kick every pile of bean straw. The other will *look* at all and kick very few. A "hunter" looks and sees! A "walker" looks and sees not.

The average upland game hunter would be amazed at the opportunities offered by a good tracking snow. He would probably be more surprised at where cottontails will find cover in time of prolonged severe weather. Their probable favorite, other than the heavy cover mentioned previously, is plowed ground. Yes, plowed ground!

Much fall plowing is done in stubble and pasture ground. As furrows are laid over and intermittently break, ideal grass-lined tunnels are formed. Such shelter attracts cottontails in time of severe cold. In mild weather, such cover is too warm and stuffy. The cottontail takes cover primarily for concealment. He is bothered only by a combination of extreme cold with the usually concurring shortage of fattening foods such as corn at that time under snow cover. Farm boys and old-time hunters pull cottontails out of these furrows with gloved hands after tracking them down.

I well recall getting ten cottontails in two hours one January morning. This was back when Illinois' daily limit was ten rabbits. We had had ten days of extreme cold with several inches of snow on the ground. Game made no tracks because of the frozen crust on the snow. On the morning after the first all-night thaw, tracking was difficult and tricky, but very rewarding. I carried a single-barrel 12-gauge that day and never used it!

There's something about a thistle. Yes, there must be something the bouncy cottontail likes about thistles. Many is the time when, leaden-footed with fatigue and coat heavy with game, I investigated one more lone Canada or bull thistle and was rewarded by kicking out a big, fat buck rabbit. It seems one never misses one like that when tired enough to be relaxed and happily aware of the heavy pull of full game pockets.

Successful trackers work in circles when encountering a heavy concentration of small game tracks. Game is rarely found in a feeding area in that spot where tracks are heaviest. Work along the edges in a rough circle and check out each track leaving the area. Game tends to bed down away from the "kitchen" and "family room." Tracks almost invariably prove this.

Rabbits like people because humans offer shelter and protection. Sounds like a strange statement, and were a rabbit capable of expressing in human tongue, he might not be in agreement with me. Who can deny that rabbits are at their most abundant on the edge of town and near farm buildings? There are two principal reasons. First, foxes, coon, and hawks, give some berth to inhabited places. In addition, buildings, junk piles, orchards, and like places give protection from even the farm dog. Farmer-owned beagles may in part have derived their doleful expressions from living in close proximity to cottontails just out of reach under every crib and hen house. Certainly most frustrating!

A good shot does not need a "cannon" to kill game. With some distress, I view the trend toward larger gauge guns and magnum loads. A couple of seasons back, I went out hunting with an acquaintance who hunts upland game and ducks in various states for a total of more than a hundred days per year. We worked a small patch of standing corn in the direction of a bare hog lot. Two rabbits jumped together almost at our feet. My companion of the afternoon blasted the first one at about eight yards and the second at about twelve yards. You guessed it! He was shooting a full-choke 12-gauge with six shot magnum loads! Most disturbing, however, was this—he did not care that those rabbits were torn to shreds and not worth cleaning. In my opinion, that fellow is not a hunter. He is a "shooter" who has yet to become a hunter.

Cottontail rabbits are hunted with weapons ranging from .22 rifles to full-choke 12-gauge guns. Of course, not all guns fit every individual or every hunting situation. Much has been written about variable chokes, automatic shotguns, and magnum loads. All have much to recommend them. I have long felt that a shotgun should, in cost and performance, be sufficient to dependably do the job that the individual hunter is attempting.

A ten-year-old boy with training and a proper attitude regarding safety can kill small game consistently and cleanly with a 410-gauge, single-barrel. For rabbits, the gun should be of modified choke. To best illustrate or prove this contention, try this. Borrow a full-choke 410 and shoot a pattern at 15 yards. Pretty small, isn't it? A young hunter will miss or cripple much game with a small-gauge, full-choke gun.

Many hunters find less and less time to hunt. A full-choke gun is not the right gun for a "rusty" shooter to use on cottontails. In fact, most hunters will do better with a modified-choke 12-gauge gun, light to medium loads, and #6 shot than they will with the same gun in full choke and heavier loads and shot. However, there is one qualification. Gut-shot rabbits die much later in holes or brush or are at the mercy of fox and crow. Your modified-choke shotgun can range in gauge in accordance with the size and weight of the shooter. Just remember that you do not need the heaviest available loads to consistently make clean kills on cottontails at reasonable range.

I used a Winchester modified '97 in 12-gauge with a 28-inch barrel modified-choke for many years. I have shot 500 rabbits with that gun. Here is how I learned to load it for the best results. In chamber 2½" shell, 1¼ drams powder, and 1 ounce #5 shot. First shell in magazine the same. Second shell in the magazine—2¾" shell, 1½ drams powder, and 1¼ ounce of #6 shot. That gave me a heavy load for that third shot when the most unusual circumstances warranted its use. Normally, a third shot is needed only to stop a cripple or after snapshot misses in heavy brush or other extreme cover.

Yes, the gun is all-important, and loads are of great importance. Learn the limitations of your weight and build to handle the size and gauge of the gun. Rely on medium range accurate shooting with adequate loads. In your double, pump, or automatic, try a very light load in the chamber and back it up with heavier loads. You will make more clean kills and stop most cripples.

Another error of many "shooters" is in attempting to "reach out" for them. When a rabbit is out at 40 yards and moving away fast, let him go! When a cock pheasant flushes at extreme range or sets his wings way off at extreme range, let him go!

Needless and foolish crippling of game is a sinful waste of one of our most precious natural resources. What name would you give to an automatic fanatic who bangs three shots at a cottontail at 50, 55, or 60 yards? Haven't you seen it done?

Use the weather to help you and learn where to hunt and when. Don't charge through the corn. Work it! Observe the wind. From what direction was it last night? Track one rabbit at a time. Too many tracks mean move out a little. Remember, rabbits like the environment created by people.

Use shells just big enough to do the job. Don't waste our precious small-game heritage. Happy hunting! ❊

The Wedding

The church and the wedding deserve mention. The church was a "turn-of-the-century" frame and block building. I believe it had plumbing. Red clay was everywhere, no walks or drives or parking. There was a big crowd for the rehearsal, wedding, and reception.

The ruggedly handsome father of the bride came to the rehearsal dressed in the absolutely appropriate attire for the area—namely, a new work shirt and blue denim bib overalls. He looked great! Mind you, this man had 12,000 acres of wheat and 2,000 cattle!

The wedding ceremony went well. Lots of people. Terrible piano. Oh, I forgot about the paint. The church inside and outside was white casein paint. Wire graveyard fence plus barbed wire was also painted white. I think that paint is made with cows' milk. I have no notion of how it is made.

You know, the whole setting, country, and lifestyle had some of the feeling of a John Wayne movie. ✽

What If I Could Walk...

Once more along the beach front of the Royal Hawaiian...
Along the beach at Maffin Bay under the sheltering palms...
Sarmi, Maffin Bay...
Across the Sigmund-Erb-McDowell farms...
Under the tracks and head out to the fields...
Up the hill to the high school on an October day...
Onto the stage with trombone in hand and win the solo contest...
Along Spring Avenue to Haggerts...
Down the alley and head for town...
Ride my Iver Johnson bike down the alley...
Across the miles back home with game pockets full...
In march time once again as first trombonist in the Decoration Day
     Parade...
From Brainard Street to Ellsworth School...
Club in hand and catch two rabbits as I moved like an Indian scout...
Climb the water tower...
Ride in the Kroehler furniture truck to ball games again...
Be a patrol boy again...
Ring the school bell just one more time...   ❋

...With His Wagon

Alittle while back I was in attendance at a local gathering, and Mrs. Harold Lehman walked up to me, gave me a big hug, and with tear-filled eyes said, "You brought Paul home..." I was momentarily at a loss for words until she added, "...with his wagon." Then I remembered.

In 1949, Laurabelle and I had built a new home at 817 North Eagle Street. The Harold Lehman family lived on Eagle Street about half a block south of our home.

It was a kid-filled neighborhood—Keith and Mary Jean Peterson and two children, Bob and Jill Eby with two kids, Gene and Marian Schum with two sons, the Ed Johnsons' four, the Peterson, Fry, Tandler, Sahs, Eby, Johnson, Schum, Lehman, Haberman and Wright families contributed about 26 kids, with many more child-filled homes in the rest of the Pilgrim Addition. Everyone pretty much knew the neighborhood kids on sight. Thank heavens this was true!

On a warm, sunny day, probably in 1951, I was driving home from downtown and as I turned off Washington Street by Kendall Park headed for Eagle Street, I saw a little boy pulling a wagon down the middle of the street. I recognized him as a Lehman. I automatically stopped, set the kid on the front seat, put his wagon in the car trunk, drove to the Lehman home, and unloaded boy and wagon in their driveway. His mile-from-home trip was ended. I got back in my car and headed for home about half a block away.

> I stopped, set the kid on the front seat, put his wagon in the trunk... His mile-from-home trip was ended!

Meanwhile, "Where's Paul?" exclaimed someone in the Lehman household.

No one knew. "When did you last see him?" asked his mother.

No one knew! "Where is his wagon?" asked John. No one knew! The search was mounting. Telephone the neighbors—big kids got on bikes to ride up and down the streets—

"Where could he be?" asked the children. No one knew!

I have one indelible memory. Pictured clearly in my mind is Paul's mother, Mrs. Lehman, sprinting down the driveway, followed by other mothers and children, all out to gather up the lost one—who was now found!

And you know what? After 45 years, that was a wonderful hug from the mother of Paul Lehman!   ❉

What If?

What if I had been awarded the Congressional Medal of Honor?

Would I have attended college?

Would I have stayed in the Army?

Would I have exploited that fame?

Who would say no to any reasonable request? Certainly not a politician or his appointees.

Might I have entered politics?

How about the pastoral ministry?

Is a Congressional Medal of Honor recipient a member of the world's most exclusive club? I suppose not—there are always ex-presidents around.

❋

Epilogue

"My dad says..." is a phrase so often used by my son in referring to me or quoting me in conversation. Picture him, if you will, in a group in animated conversation almost squirming, eyes sparkling as he waits to speak, and finally gets the chance to say, "My dad says..."

I did not really understand or comprehend his total acceptance of my daily word until one day not long ago I was looking at his senior high school yearbook, and there under his individual class roster picture are the words, "My Dad Says..."

That good-looking, bright, high-school senior quoting me is now John Alan Fry, a head of a family and an urbane, active community leader. Today, John Alan Fry is a most respected church, family, and community business leader.

Only one thing has changed. My grandchildren tell me that Alan and the family now say, "*Grandpa* says..."

As all of my sons would say, "That's fine!"   ✳

The John Fry family